CADOGAN
guides

lazy days out
in the loire

KT-434-530

Cadogan Books plc
27–29 Berwick Street
London W1V 3RF, UK

guides@cadogan.demon.co.uk

**Distributed in the USA by
The Globe Pequot Press**
6 Business Park Road, PO Box 833,
Old Saybrook, Connecticut 06475-0833

Copyright © Philippe Barbour 1997
Illustrations © Charles Shearer 1997
Book, cover and map design by Animage
Cover photography and illustration
  by Horatio Monteverde
Maps © Cadogan Guides, designed by Animage
  and drawn by Map Creation Ltd

Series editor: Rachel Fielding
Editor: Linda McQueen
Cookery editor: Michelle Clark

Production: Book Production Services
Printed and bound in the UK by Redwood Books Ltd , Trowbridge

ISBN 1-86011-037-1
A catalogue record for this book is available
from the British Library

*The author and publishers have made every effort to ensure the accuracy of
the information in the book at the time of going to press. However, they
cannot accept any responsibility for any loss, injury or inconvenience resulting
from the use of information contained in this guide.*

About the Author

Philippe Barbour is the author of the *Cadogan Guide to the Loire* and *Lazy Days Out in Provence*, as well as co-author of *Wine Buyer's Guide: Saint Emilion*. He recently edited the *European Union Handbook* (published by Fitzroy Dearborn) and is now preparing the *Cadogan Guide to Brittany*.

Acknowledgements

I would like to thank Kate Berney, David Lamb, John Herbert and Andrew Cotton, who all helped in the strenuous researching of good restaurants for this guide. At the same time I would also like to apologize to them for the weight they claim to have put on in trying to help me. Yes, it was a job that inevitably involved some suffering. In all we tried scores and scores of restaurants to bring you this selection.

I would like to thank many of the people who work in tourism in the *départements* along the Loire for their assistance: in the Indre, Nicole Gasquet; in the Loir valley, Loïc Rousseau; in the Orléanais, Anne-Marie Leforestier; in the Loir-et-Cher, Sylvia Fromenteaud and Carole; in Touraine, Damien Dejoie, Frank Artiges, Pierre Sabouraud and Jean-Louis Sureau; in Anjou, Hélène Ramsamy, Valérie Brun and Dominique Dubois; in Loire Atlantique, Paul Ligtenberg.

Please help us keep this guide up to date

Every effort has been made to ensure the accuracy of the information in this book at the time of going to press. However, standards in restaurants and practical details such as opening times and, in particular, prices are liable to change. We would be delighted to receive any comments concerning existing entries or indeed any suggestions for inclusion in future editions or companion volumes. Significant contributions will be acknowledged in the next edition, and authors of the best letters will receive a copy of the Cadogan Guide of their choice.

Contents

Introduction

Stags' antlers, stork and hedgehog—these are delicacies that you're unlikely to find on a menu in the Loire nowadays, although they were apparently cooked up for the delectation of Loire French kings in centuries past. Freshwater fish, game and goat's cheese, such are the mainstays of the region's cuisine that will crop up time and again across the Loire Valley, along with its wonderful fruit and vegetables. There's no better picture to advertise the magnificent fertility and diversity of the valley's soil than the kitchen garden of Villandry, where vegetable growing has been turned into art.

For a picture of Loire feasting in centuries past, were you to go by the diet of Gargantua, Rabelais' comical giant hero, you'd expect to be served cartloads of tripe at every meal, a dozen hams, fish egg paste and shovelfuls of mustard thrown in, all washed down with your personal barrel or two of wine. Although many of the principal dishes of Loire cooking have remained fixed for some time, with many references in Rabelais to fish and meat specialities that you will find today, you'll be relieved to hear that the traditional cuisine has been lightened somewhat.

Moving on to more recent culinary silliness, the worst experimental excesses and sometimes mean-spirited notions of *nouvelle cuisine* did turn the heads of some chefs across the region in the 1970s, but nowadays you're not that likely to be served a tiny portion of *sandre à la fraise*. Not that experimentation is frowned upon. On the contrary: several of the chefs recommended here do attempt seriously to add new touches and variations to Loire cuisine. Most of the restaurants in this guide have been selected, however, because they concentrate on careful preparation of the good old traditional Loire dishes with fine fresh ingredients.

Location was a major consideration in our choice of restaurants. Many of them lie close to rivers or right on the waterfront. The Loire Valley isn't simply about the Loire river itself. The region has just about the most extensive network of tributaries in France. Here we've found delightful riverbank seats by the Loiret, Indre and Maine, as well as one address right by the Canal d'Orléans. We haven't ignored the Loire either. Near Blois we watched herons in the water while we ate and at the Anjou *guinguettes* we could see cormorants diving for their food as we were served ours.

Our stop in Troo combines many of the delights of these parts of France in one place. The village sits above the Loir river (not the Loire). From its heights you get some of the most gorgeous valley views imaginable, while if you clamber down the narrow paths in the hillside, you pass in front of troglodyte houses. The riverbanks across the Loire Valley proved a rich vein for quarrying stone. And then the empty caverns left behind were converted into storage rooms, wine cellars, mushroom farms, even troglodyte homes. The troglodyte theme is one of the best concealed attractions of the Loire Valley.

Many of our restaurants are in wine-making territories too. Touraine and Anjou are best known as the most successful grounds for Loire wines. The complexity of these wine areas has sometimes meant that their diversity of production has simply been ignored. Anjou has found it really difficult to shake off the very unfair image of simply producing sweet rosé. Yet Anjou still produces excellent reds like Saumur-Champigny and some of the Anjou-Villages, the celebratory Saumur Mousseux sparkling wines, superlative sweet whites in Bonnezeaux and Quarts-de-Chaume in the Coteaux du Layon, and one of the great dry white wines of western France, Savennières. Sancerre and Muscadet are extraordinarily well known abroad by contrast with these names. They lie at the limits of the territories we cover in our 20 lazy days out. But what of the wines of the Cher valley, of Cheverny, Valençay, Jasnières and the Loir valley? On a visit to the greater Loire Valley you can make many viticultural discoveries.

We've said that virtually all the restaurants we've chosen are in lovely, typical Loire Valley settings. They're close to the châteaux, churches, rivers, forests and vineyards that give the area such wide appeal. But we've taken a pretty broad interpretation of the Loire Valley here, starting in the east with Sancerre, on the old province of Berry's border with Burgundy, the Loire river the frontier between the two. (The source of the river is hundreds of miles south) We head on westwards along the great *fleuve*, through the Orléanais, home of the Capetian kings, through the Valois territories of the Blésois and Touraine, and on into Anjou, homeland of the Plantagenets, before reaching the once-great port of Nantes in the Loire Atlantique. But we also stray into areas on the periphery of the Loire. Valençay, like Sancerre, is in the northern territories of the old province of the Berry. Troo and the forest of Bercé are by the Loir, in some ways a much less touristy miniature version of the Loire valley. We also dip into the Sologne, the great sandy, heathery forest below the Loire's most northerly arc.

Visiting the Loire generally involves visiting a fair number of châteaux. We thought it only fair to recommend a brace of beautiful ones where you can actually stop and eat fantastically, rather than being ejected by ferocious guides at lunchtime. And these chateaux' lunchtime menus aren't outrageously priced compared with many big city restaurants. That said, several other of the addresses we've included do offer bargain value good food, so there's a good mix of prices.

One of the great attractions for the kings and aristocrats who built their châteaux along the Loire Valley was the large number of forests teeming with game. Several impressively large forests remain. Their presence has a profound effect on restaurant menus in the autumn—game and mushrooms suddenly feature much more prominently. Menus will vary according to the time of year you go. Fresh river fish of course put in their appearance in season. Salmon rarely make it up river nowadays, but eels are still caught in good number. *Sandre*, flagfish of Loire cuisine, though, is more likely to come from eastern Europe than from the Loire these days.

The Loire Valley is often considered by French people as a fairly conservative, stick-in-the-mud region, where bourgeois tradition triumphs. This isn't quite a fair view. With the countless centuries of great river trading along the Loire and its tributaries—the Greeks may have traded with the Cornish via the Loire—the region has long been open to outside influences. Nantes, our most westerly stop, was one of the great ports in the days of Ancien Régime empire, its stunning buildings gracefully constructed on the back of the disgraceful slave trade. Exotic spices and luxury goods would be shipped back here to delight the wealthy in search of novelties. By chance, the last two restaurants are among the most experimental in this guide with their exotic touches, one even adding Japanese elements to several dishes. The Loire, they demonstrate, is still open to outside influences as well as maintaining its very traditional French side.

Sancerre's Vines of Success

Auberge du Vigneron

The success of the Sancerrois's vineyards means that the goats that used to graze here in large numbers have been pushed westwards into the Pays Fort since the 1950s. Both these areas are beautifully hilly and pop up as quite a surprise after the flat lands to the south. Coming north along the Loire to Sancerre gives you a particularly marvellous shock as the sensuous hills make their sudden seductive appearance.

The hilltop town of Sancerre dominates the Sancerrois with its magical views down on to the Loire. Here the river serves as the border between the old provinces of Berry to the west and Burgundy to the east. On the opposite bank of the river from Sancerre lies another famous Loire wine region: Pouilly Fumé, in Burgundy. There are some highly reputed wine producers with cellars in Sancerre itself, but the winemakers' villages in the valleys around it make a very enjoyable tour. Although the goats may have been moved westwards, it is still possible to visit a goat's cheese producer in the Sancerrois. Chavignol is the king of the *crottins*, the affectionate name (meaning droppings) given to the cheeses around here.

South of Sancerre lies another hilly and fine wine-producing area, Menetou-Salon, much less well-known than its famous neighbour, but well worth exploring. The village of La Borne close to Menetou-Salon has been wholly colonised by potters.

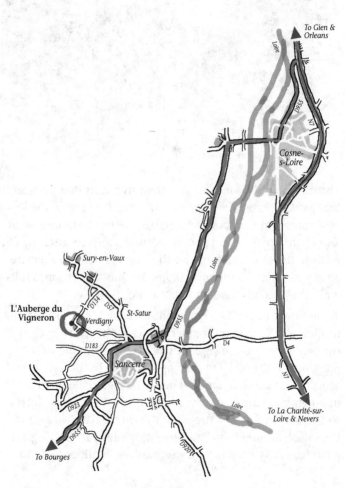

To get to Sancerre, if you're coming from Paris you can head south down the A7 motorway and then join the N7—or take the N7 all the way from the capital to avoid motorway tolls. The N7 eventually joins the Loire and goes along the river passing opposite Sancerre. This road is busy and not particularly picturesque, so cross at Gien to enjoy a slightly nicer journey along the west bank. If you're coming off the A71 motorway joining Orléans and Bourges, exit at Bourges, head a few kilometres along the N151 in the direction of La Charité-sur-Loire and then branch off north-eastwards on the D955 to Sancerre.

To reach L'Auberge du Vigneron after a visit to the hilltop town of Sancerre, you need to head down to the lower part of town. Once down below, follow the signs for St-Satur briefly. Soon you should take a left turn northwards towards Sury-en-Vaux on the D57. But you only stay on that road a couple of hundred metres before turning west for Verdigny. A winding route through beautiful sloping vineyards leads you to this little village which spreads slightly chaotically into the vines. Follow the clear bottle-shaped signs for the village museum and the Auberge du Vigneron so as not to get lost in the little labyrinth of streets.

L'Auberge du Vigneron

L'Auberge du Vigneron, Verdigny-en-Sancerre, 18300 Sancerre, © 02 48 79 38 68. Closed Wed. Annual closure Dec. Menus at 89F and 119F.

After feasting your eyes on the views of vineyards and the Loire from Sancerre town, you'll find the Auberge du Vigneron tucked away in its village at the foot of Sancerrois hills. The restaurant is small, set off a little yard, with barn-like doors in its roof of old brown tiles.

There are two small dining rooms; the decoration in the main, beamed dining room is simple, sometimes basic, sometimes mildly amusing, sometimes slightly tacky. There's a bar perched on barrels near the entrance, and an oven, football cups, pictures of vines and horses, a chiming clock with weights provided by wine bottles, and fake grape bunches here and there. The second dining room is a dark, low-vaulted, quite atmospheric little chamber. You sit down on ordinary French kitchen chairs in front of tablecloths of simple paper, the condiments in basic plastic servers. French radio muzak may be playing, but conversation at the tables around should be lively. This is a local favourite. The restaurant-cum-bed-and-breakfast turns out to be a parish venture.

The menus are extremely good value, both four courses. And you'll find a good number of choices of both hors d'œuvre and main dishes even on the cheaper menu. Having said that, you may find that the starters are dominated by goat's cheese *crottins*, while the predominance of sauces *au Sancerre*, with Sancerre wine, among the *plats de résistance* may seem almost comical. You might find yourself with the choice between *poulet au Sancerre*, *saumon sauce Sancerre*, *pintade* (guinea-fowl) *au Sancerre*, *canard* (duck) *au Sancerre* and *andouillette* (sausage) *au Sancerre*! And the *faux filet sauce vigneronne* looks suspiciously like a familiar dish by another name. We wondered whether the water would come *au Sancerre*.

While struggling over the choices, you will naturally want to taste some Sancerre by way of apéritif. Sancerre is known far and wide for its fine crisp white wine—from the Sauvignon blanc grape variety, frequently with definite hints of gooseberries—but it also produces a small amount of red. This you could try in the house apéritif, mixed with a little dose of *crème de mûre*, blackberry liqueur. This lovely fragrant and fruity drink, mixing red wine with red liqueur, is referred to on the menu as a *kir berrichon*, but is also humorously known to some as a 'communiste', the name it was once given by a French president entertaining a Soviet leader! Wine is rarely cheap in French restaurants. Here even the generic Sancerre, either *blanc*, *rouge* or *rosé*, came at 98F a bottle, 58F the half bottle. The light-coloured reds, from Pinot Noir, can be delicately fruity.

Wine crept into one of our starters, the superb *œufs en meurette*, actually a dish associated with Burgundy, but that province lies only just across the Loire waters from Sancerre. This is one of the very tastiest ways to serve eggs, an extremely satisfying soup of a recipe. You may feel you need a whole extra baguette to lap up all the sauce. Alternatively, it would make good sense to try the Sancerrois's other great culinary speciality, local goat's cheese, as an hors d'œuvre. You could go for a *crottin chaud* with salad, or an *omelette au crottin*. But perhaps the best is the *feuilleté de crottin*, goat's cheese in flaky pastry, served up with salad containing plenty of garlic and walnuts. *Noix* is both the generic word for nuts and the specific word for walnuts in French; walnut trees were once grown widely in the province of Berry and are still to be found in patches.

On to some of those main dishes with Sancerre wine. A formidable knife was provided for the *poulet au Sancerre*, but it was totally unnecessary as the chicken fell off the bone without effort. The wine sauce was again thick as with the *œufs en meurette* (avoid ordering two wine sauces in a row). You could opt for simple dishes such as a grilled skewer of lamb, a steak served with shallots, or trout in a sorrel sauce, or, if you are feeling adventurous, for *cervelle au beurre* (brains in butter). There was one traitor to Sancerre in the group, *filet de canard au Cognac*.

Goat is almost always going to be the star of any cheeseboard along the Loire Valley. In this case the board takes the form of a little cheese basket. The type of goat's cheese you may not be familiar with here is very fresh cheese which you spoon out of a pot onto your plate and, following tradition, eat with raw shallots. Worth a try and quite a potent mix of tastes.

Tarte Tatin is a pudding you'll find on virtually every menu on the Loire. It was actually 'invented' at Lamotte-Beuvron in the lake and forest land of the Sologne which lies not far west of the Sancerrois. Many of the versions can be sickly-sweet, but at the Auberge du Vigneron it was pleasantly light, the apples cut like shallots, with a chewily caramel top. Or you might opt for fresh strawberries if they're in season, or, sticking doggedly to Sancerre's wine theme, *prunes au vin*, plums in wine, a fitting end to a Sancerrois meal.

tartetatin

Oeufs en Meurette

*Served as a starter, the eggs look and taste very good set on slices of toast.
For a special touch, you could use shaped cutters to make large croûtons.*

Serves 2 as a main course, 4 as a starter

2 shallots or 1 small onion, finely chopped
2 rashers smoked bacon, diced
1 tablespoon oil
2 medium carrots, diced
1 tablespoon plain flour
1 litre/1 ¾ pints strong red wine (e.g. Gamay)
150ml/¼ pint jellied veal stock or reduced chicken stock
1 bouquet garni
1 tablespoon chopped fresh parsley
½ tablespoon chopped fresh thyme
4 eggs
salt and pepper

*Brown the shallots or onion and the diced smoked bacon in the oil. Add the
carrots, flour, wine, stock, bouquet garni, parsley and thyme and season to
taste. Leave to simmer gently, half covered, for 1 hour over a low heat.
Meanwhile, just before the sauce is ready, poach the eggs either in an egg
poacher or by breaking them, 2 at a time, into boiling water with
1 tablespoon of vinegar added. Then place 2 eggs on each plate if serving
as a main course, 1 if as a starter, and pour the sauce around them.*

---

touring around

The praises of **Sancerre**, the famous Loire white wine, are so widely
sung that often the beauty of Sancerre the town and its magnificent
site is passed over rather too quickly. Sancerre's old centre is really the
major dramatic stop on the Berry bank of the Loire. The views from
Sancerre down onto the river are spectacular, particularly towards the
south, where the Loire tapers away into the distance through a magical landscape that wouldn't look amiss in a late-medieval painting.
Down by the Loire lies the lower town of St-Satur, its silo sticking out
rather discordantly. Far to the north, you can sometimes make out the

huge chimneys of the nuclear power station of Belleville-sur-Loire, churning artificial clouds of vapour into the sky.

The houses of Sancerre have been pushed together on the hilltop as though they were a terrible inconvenience, a patch taken over by people while vines can otherwise grow undisturbed all around. On the pinnacle of the hill, one tower is set apart in its own clump of trees. This Tour des Fiefs constitutes the last vestige of the former château which protected this historically important strategic post, in French royal hands during the Hundred Years War. Across the waters of the Loire lay the enemy, the Burgundians, in league with the vile English.

To wander around Sancerre, the best place to park is close to the esplanade of La Porte César and the entrance to the château. It is then an easy walk into the main square. Sancerre doesn't have any major cultural sites. The remaining tower of the château is rarely open *(only Sun and bank holidays pm, March–Oct)*. The breathtaking views are the best the town has to offer. Wander off down some of the steep streets that lead away from the main square. The biggest attractions are the barn-door-sized entrances, opened for the vineyard crops. The two big wine-making houses to visit in Sancerre itself are Mellot and Vacheron. As well as the wines, other specialities you can find in town include the *crottins de chèvre,* the *croquets de Sancerre* biscuits and local stoneware (*grès*) pottery.

The lines of vines reach up and stretch round the town and the surrounding hillsides like glorious patterned cloth. A tour of the **Sancerrois wine villages** is well worthwhile in the morning, either to go and sample wine at various cellars or to enjoy the scenery. A suggested short tour would be to head west to Amigny, then south to Venoize and Bué. Go west once more to Crézancy and then head back towards Sancerre via Reigny. Then cut across to Les Champions and down to **Chavignol**. If you want to see goat's cheese being made in Chavignol, however, you'll need to head there early. You won't find the goats around the village, but their milk is transported here to be transformed into various cheeses and in the mornings you can follow the production processes at the *fromagerie* in the village centre. Back in **Verdigny**, around lunchtime, the best wine estate to visit is that of André Dezat, a local figure known as *le petit Dé* and one of the most influential men responsible for bringing Sancerre its postwar success.

In the afternoon, head slightly southwest from Sancerre. You need to find your way on to the D22 leading to La Borne and Henrichemont. **La Borne** has four different elements of interest to tourists: the pottery museum in a former chapel; the contemporary ceramics centre in the former girls' school; the Musée Vassil Ivanoff dedicated to that accomplished potter; and the numerous present-day potters with their houses-cum-showrooms dotted around the parish—they seem to have taken over most of La Borne's properties and are almost as tightly packed together here as pieces in a kiln.

The pottery tradition goes back quite some time in the area. A 1627 contract between the Loire boatmen and the potters of Neuvy-les-Deux-Clochers (a little east of La Borne) shows that the vast majority of production was being shipped down the Loire to Nantes by this period—pieces have been found as far away as Montreal! Evidence has also been found for pottery-making dating back to the 13th century. The place to learn about the history of La Borne pottery is in the former chapel, converted into a pottery museum, its floor covered with lovely kiln bricks marked by their contact with salt and wood ash. In the church collection you can admire some fine pieces by the Talbot family, who prospered by making Toby jug-type pieces and figurative works, in particular in the shape and attire of 19th-century women.

Go to the Centre de Céramique next to the church to see the rich variety of some of the work of the contemporary potters, filled with inventiveness and eccentricity. The individual styles are very distinct. Looking at the displays is a good way of seeing if there are particular potters you might like to visit from over 40 in the village association—the people at the museum can then tell you whether a visit is possible and will supply a parish map and directions.

One of the first of the new wave of artistic potters to arrive at La Borne after the Second World War was Vassil Ivanoff, in 1946. He worked here almost 30 years until his death. The collection of works by him in the Musée Vassil Ivanoff is placed in one small room in a village cottage, worth a browse through. The oxblood-red glazes, almost like rich blackcurrant or blackberry jam, attract the attention first, but then the variety of his sculptural forms emerges.

Pot Luck by the Canal d'Orléans

À la Fortune du Pot

To the east of Orléans, the enormous forest of Orléans shadows the most northerly arc of the Loire. The Canal d'Orléans cuts through the middle of the forest and it's along the canal's banks rather than the Loire's that we stop for lunch.

The Loire Valley around Orléans is comically nicknamed 'Cosmetics Valley' because of the number of beauty companies that have settled here. The main tourist attraction of the Forêt d'Orléans, the Château de Chamerolles, a largely newly con-coted castle, has dedicated itself to scent and toiletries. You can even try to invent a perfume of your own there.

The great attractions are by the Loire itself. The abbey church of St-Benoît-sur-Loire is one of the most famous and histori-cally significant spots in French Christianity, one of its most important medieval edifices. Just east of St-Benoît, the splendid Château de Sully mirrors itself narcissistically in the Loire. This beautiful stretch of the Loire river is also frequently referred to as the Val d'Or. If you prefer to concentrate on the river rather than sightseeing, there are stretches you can easily stroll along here, while a crammed little museum at Châteauneuf-sur-Loire pays homage to the Loire sailors of centuries past.

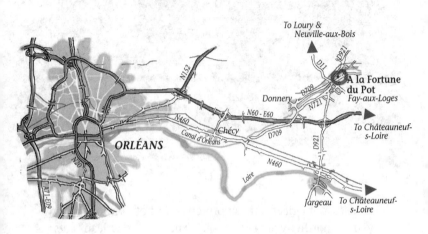

getting there

Looking at the general Michelin map of France, find Jargeau, around 20km east of Orléans, on the south bank of the Loire. Fay-aux-Loges is 6 or 7km north of Jargeau along the D921, so north of the Loire. It's also a little way north of the N60, the main road connecting Orléans with Châteauneuf-sur-Loire. If you're coming off the A71 motorway, take the Orléans North exit and follow signs for Châteauneuf-sur-Loire, getting on to the N60 to reach the restaurant. Go to the centre of the village of Fay to find A La Fortune du Pot. Don't cross to the north side of the Canal d'Orléans, but just before the road-bridge over it, turn right and you come to the short lane leading to the car park for the restaurant.

A la Fortune du Pot

A la Fortune du Pot, 2 chemin de Halage, 45450 Fay-aux-Loges, ✆ 02 38 59 56 54, 🖷 02 38 57 04 25. Closed Tues eve, Wed and Sun eve. Annual holidays early–mid-Aug and Feb school holidays. Menus at 115F, 155F, 178F, 180F and 245F.

From among the working-class grey and beige roughcast houses of Fay-aux-Loges, the village church spire protrudes like a rocket. The restaurant is in one of the prettiest houses in Fay, a canal-side *chaumière* or thatched house. The street address, *chemin de Halage*, is the French for towpath. The houses on the other side of the canal aren't so pretty, but lilies and moorhens on the water help make up for that. You may find the towpath inviting enough for a walk later, but A La Fortune du Pot separates its grounds from the public way by a string of garland-shaped chains.

To one side of the restaurant's car park, behind turquoise-tinted cypresses, the owner has made use of some ruins to create a garden, former walls providing divides. The odd fruit tree grows in this patch of land and tables are set out here for summer—you could take an apéritif in this strange garden. On the other side of the car park, a few dining tables may be laid out in the simple conservatory. The main dining room is spacious and if you look up at the ceiling beams you'll see row upon row of plates, their patterns copying various styles of pottery from across France. The house apparently once served as a wine storage cellar. You can imagine barrels being loaded and unloaded in centuries past from barges on the canal. Interesting culinary objects decorate various corners of the dining room. The most bizarre greets you at the door: a *batteur de pâtissier.* This contraption once helped the traditional French cake makers to prepare their mixtures and is basically the most complicated hand-worked whisk imaginable, seemingly invented by a mad scientist. It makes you realize the genius of the modern electric mixer. The most tasteless touch in the restaurant's decoration is an item that crops up all too regularly across the hunting-mad Loire Valley, the type of chandelier where the bulbs sit among deer hooves and antlers. But the feel at A La Fortune du Pot is generally warm and light.

You will find Orléanais wine on the menu. You may prefer to opt for something a little more sophisticated, but the local *vin délimité de qualité supérieure* does offer good value. The cheerful, chirpy *maître d'hôtel*-cum-wine waiter who served us, Jean-Michel Lemoyne, can certainly help you with your choice. He can speak English if you like. He says he even practised it for a short while at one of London's top restaurants, Le Gavroche. He throws the odd quip into his conversation and calls A La Fortune du Pot his Waterside Inn. The owner, Hervé Fouquiau, is also the *chef de cuisine.*

The expression *à la fortune du pot* normally implies taking pot luck with a meal, but the name is of course ironic and the cooking here is reliably good. The 115F menu already offered four courses, but if you went for the weekday lunchtime menu at 155F you'd get more choices and several extras thrown in—an *amuse gueule,* coffee to end with, and in between, a quarter litre of either white or red wine. If you go for the cheapest menu, your only choice comes with the puddings, so you may feel a bit restricted by that. However, the *galantine de cannette au foie de volaille et ses raisins secs,* a thin but chocolatey-rich slice of pressed duck and liver, followed by a steak with an Orléanais sauce (the Orléanais was as reputed for its vinegar as its wine in times past, and this piquant sauce combines vinegar with mustard), cheese and salad, and either profiteroles, a tart or a mix of sorbets or ice-creams for pudding makes for a very creditable meal. The day we ate here the *entrecôte* was also covered with a generous portion of chanterelle mushrooms and served with French beans tied together into a sheaf by a piece of bacon: there are humorous touches to the presentation as well as care in the cuisine.

You'll be much more spoilt with the 178F menu than the more basic one. S*andre,* is a freshwater fish almost synonymous with Loire cuisine. Now *sandre,* or zander, or pikeperch, as it is variously referred to, can be somewhat dry and bland, so it needs a good sauce to pep it up. The most usual way to do this is with a *beurre blanc,* the Loire Valley sauce *par excellence*, made with shallots, butter, white wine and wine vinegar. At A La Fortune du Pot the *sandre* starter is often mixed with salmon and lobster in a *terrine* covered in an orangey-coloured tomato coulis. The tomato taste isn't overdone, and you can even detect the odd little denser flavour of lobster. This might be followed by salmon in sorrel, another typical Loire sauce, or steak.

The more expensive menus consist of five courses. Fish features largely on all. You might start with the zander *terrine* described above, and follow with *ravioli de truite au basilic*. The pasta is homemade and somehow the trout filling has a meaty consistency. Not only basil flavours the dish. Hints of shallots, Noilly-Prat (a type of vermouth or aromatic wine) and mint come into the sauce made with fish stock. A curious red purée accompanies the dish, the potatoes mixed with a third of beetroot. All rather refined and delicious. Bass fillet is served with an even more daring sauce. *Badiane* is star anis, which can add a fizz to dishes. After these three bold fish dishes you reach the reassurance of cheese and pudding.

It's only with the two most expensive menus that you get the full choice of puddings. So you'd need to go for one of these to taste the recipe given below. This is an ideal autumn dish and pears are one of the great specialities of the Loire Valley, in the Orléanais and in Anjou in particular. The top of the pudding, in the shape of a pear, had the colour of a leaf falling from a tree.

Feuilleté de Poire Caramélisé au Miel

Serves 4

250g/9oz puff pastry
75g/3oz caster sugar
500ml/17fl oz water
6 pears, peeled and cored
15g/½oz unsalted butter
85ml/3fl oz pear eau-de-vie or brandy
135g/4¾ acacia or other runny honey
400ml/14fl oz single cream
icing sugar, for dusting
4 fresh mint leaves, to decorate (optional)

Roll the pastry out to about a 5mm/¼in thickness and cut it into 4 equal-sized pieces and, if you like, into pear shapes. Add the sugar to the water in

a saucepan and bring to the boil. Add the pears to the pan, reduce the heat a little and leave to cook until just tender. Preheat the oven to 230°C/450°F (gas mark 8).

Place the pastry shapes on a lightly greased baking sheet and bake in the preheated oven for 15–20 minutes. Meanwhile, put the butter into a frying pan and heat it gently until it is golden. While the butter is heating, remove the pears from the syrup and cut them into thin slices. Fry the pear slices until they turn a light brown. Add the eau-de-vie or brandy and flambé, then add the honey and cook until the pears caramelise, turning a beautiful golden colour. Add the cream and cook until the sauce is smooth.

Warm the plates in the oven. Very carefully, cut the pastry pieces in half through the middle, from side to side, to retain the pear shape, if you've shaped them. Put the lower halves of the pastry shapes on to the warmed plates, cover them with the pears and their sauce, then cover with the top halves of pastry. Sift a little icing sigar over each serving and place a fresh mint leaf on top of each pastry shape, if using, to decorate. The chef recommends serving this heavenly dessert with a semi-sweet Montlouis wine.

---

touring around

Visit the Château de Sully and the abbey church of St-Benoît in the morning. Although the landscape is flat and unwooded around Sully-sur-Loire, the **Château de Sully** (*open 16 June–15 Sept, 10–6; May–15 June and 16 Sept–Oct, 10–12 and 2–6; Mar, April and Nov, 10–12 and 2–5*) makes one of the most beautiful pictures along the whole of the Loire, romantic with its watery reflection, yet sturdy towered, the pepper-pot tops a model of their medieval kind (OK, actually rebuilt in 1908). The château's stone, originally from Briare—and nowadays replaced during restoration work with blocks from Nevers, as the first source has dried up—is a bright greyish white.

Three great families owned the Château de Sully. From the 10th to the 14th centuries it was the barons of Sully. Maurice Sully was from this family, the bishop who went off to order the building of one of France's most famous cathedrals, Notre-Dame in Paris. Then the dukes of La Trémoille transformed the place, living here from the end of the 14th century to the start of the 17th. The rectangular Vieux Château giving onto the Loire, a tower on each corner, was ordered by the first dukes of this family. The Hundred Years War was raging when work began on the great keep for Marie de Sully and her husband Guy de la Trémoille. They had a fine architect, though, the plans being by Raymond du Temple, responsible in Paris for the remodelling of the Louvre for Charles V and for the Château de Vincennes. Joan of Arc's lightning campaign against the English was halted after victory at Patay, when the Lorraine upstart was kept here against her will by the fractious Georges de la Trémoille, son of Guy and favourite of Charles VII—not all the French were fans of the Maid of Orléans. In 1602 the château became the property of Maximilien de Béthune, one of the greatest ministers in French history, working in the service of King Henri IV. He received the title of duc de Sully, but French history prefers to refer to him simply and reverentially as 'le Grand Sully'. His descendants lived here until they sold the château to the *département* of the Loiret in 1962.

Since the time the *département* bought it, the château has been considerably restored, with work still continuing. Despite this, you are allowed to visit almost the entire building. The château was practically empty in 1962; the new administration has been progressively buying up pieces linked to Sully to embellish its rooms, some of which are on a vast scale.

Dominating the sweep of the Loire known as the Val d'Or or Golden Valley and the plain around it, the **church of the abbey of St-Benoît** (*open every day outside services, 10–11.40 and 3–5.40. Closed first Friday in each month. Gregorian plainchant mass at 12 on weekdays, 11 on weekends and special days. Adm free, but the monks are grateful for donations as they have to pay for much of the upkeep of the building*) is reached from Sully via the D60, which follows the Loire's course for a time. This church, a massive structure in light Loire stone topped by black slate, dates from the 11th to the 13th centuries, with the inevitable later alterations. The history of the foundation goes much further back, into the Dark Ages.

In the course of the 7th century, around 672, a band of monks who had settled into life at a recently founded Benedictine abbey at the place named Fleury by the Loire decided to go in search of the bones of the saintly Benedict (Benoît in French), the Italian of the first half of the 6th century who had founded the great western European monastic order named after him. He had died at his monastery of Monte Cassino near Naples around 547, but this had been destroyed by Lombards in 580. The group from Fleury went all the way to Monte Cassino to scour the ground and recover what they could find of Benedict's remains. They carried back to their abbey on the Loire what they claimed to be Benedict's bones. Outraged Italian monks protested at this action, but a papal declaration accepted that the remains should stay at Fleury. The abbey consequently became an extremely venerated site in Western Christendom.

The abbey of St-Benoît amassed large territories and wealth. The early Capetian kings were generous patrons in the 11th and 12th centuries, the period in which much of the church you see was built. The crypt and the choir that stand today were begun during King Philippe I's reign, around 1070, and the choir was consecrated in 1108, the year of Philippe I's death. The great carved narthex at the entrance, originally separate from the church, is even earlier, from near the start of the 11th century. The massive monastic ensemble that grew up to the south was wiped out during the Revolution. The abbey church is perhaps more impressive than beautiful, the weight of its history and symbolism adding substantially to its gravity. Architectural historians consider it to be one of the most important of Romanesque churches in France and this because of a handful of distinctive elements. The most outstanding of these is undoubtedly the early 11th-century narthex with its famed capital carvings, very early and powerful images of Romanesque art; then come the choir and transept from later in the same century, with solid pillars and a mosaic floor reproducing a Byzantine model; and the crypt, darkly Romanesque and deeply sober, holding the remains of St Benedict which drew so many pilgrims in the Middle Ages. Philippe I's tomb also lies in the church.

In the afternoon you might head for the Château de Chamerolles. The easiest route from Fay-aux-Loges is to travel north through the Forêt d'Orléans via Sully-la-Chapelle and the D921. Where this meets the D109, turn west for the château. The **Château de Chamerolles** (*open April-Sept, 10–6; Oct–Mar, 10–5, closed Jan; closed Fri throughout the year*), a Sleeping Beauty of a building, was brought back to life in a commercial fairy-tale kind of way...or it might be a more appropriate description to say that it was revived by strong smelling salts, as the place has been transformed in good part into a museum about perfumes. The Comité Départemental du Loiret has pumped in the money (having bought the château from the Paris town council for a symbolic one franc), seemingly supported by some of the big-name perfume manufacturers who have their factories in the Loiret. Every year an exhibition takes place on a different perfumery.

The rooms concentrate on *toilette* over the centuries and in particular research into the refinement of a sweetly scented atmosphere. There's a representative section for each of the 16th, 17th, 18th and 19th centuries. The word *toilette*, a guide explains, comes from the French word *toile*, meaning cloth—scent used to be put on a piece of linen, not on clothes; the guide further admonishes visitors, saying that it's quite wrong to apply perfume directly to the skin.

Perfume bottles would start to be mass-produced at the end of the 19th century, contributing their own share of glamour to the marketing of scent. Much of the visit is devoted to the superb design work which has gone into perfume bottles across the 20th century, with stars like Lalique at the beginning. In the château's attics an atmospheric display starts with a perfumer's cabinet stocked with hundreds of essences (provided by Dior) from which perfumes can be assembled. The great creators of perfumes are known rather unflatteringly as '*nez*', noses, a name they dislike. Apparently still some 80 per cent of the '*nez*' working for the big names are French proboscises. You can amuse yourselves by sitting at the desk and concocting your own number, or by testing each other on recognizing the different scents provided, a mixture of natural and artificial ones. Would-be amateur inventors at times clog up this area.

Joan's Orléans and the Orléanais' Loiret

Orléans and its region, the Orléanais, are where Joan of Arc knew her greatest triumphs. In May 1429 it was thanks to her dogged determination that the city was liberated from a terrible long-drawn-out English siege in one of the greatest events in the Hundred Years War. Joan became known as the Maid of Orléans, and she went on to inspire a string of victories across the Orléanais.

We stick to the city of Orléans and its southern suburbs for this day out. You could visit the museums which pay tribute to Joan in the city. The Maison Jeanne d'Arc is a small affair, with models recreating important events in her life and lots of Joan of Arc commemorative plates. The Hôtel Groslot, the town hall, also contains statues and paintings aplenty of her.

However, you can see rather finer art in Orléans's Musée des Beaux-Arts. Rarely for the Loire, the collections feature mainly

Le Rivage

distinguished 17th- and 18th-century artists. Orléans suffered badly from bombing in the Second World War, and the cathedral itself has known its fair share of ups and downs. The medieval structure wasn't destroyed by foreigners, but by French Huguenots in France's vicious 16th-century religious civil wars or Guerres de Religion. It was rebuilt in Gothic style well after the Gothic period is generally considered to have ended, on the orders of the reconciling French king, Henri IV. The airy, soaring towers of the cathedral dominate the town's skyline, but have not been appreciated by all. Proust apparently compared them not to his beloved *madeleines* but to strawberry gâteaux. Perhaps the greatest pieces of art to be found in Orléans are the bronze animals at the Hôtel Cabu, inspired by Celtic gods.

The geographical and administrative region of the Orléanais was renamed the Loiret when it was reduced in scale to become a *département* at the Revolution. The French *départements* were generally named after local rivers, and the Loiret is a very short river that flows from a little south of Orléans to join the Loire some 30 kilometres to the west. Technically speaking, the Loiret is a resurgence rather than a separate river. Water from the Loire which has escaped underground east of Orléans and been supplemented by underground streams suddenly pops its head out of the ground at the uninventively named La Source. We go close to the source of the Loiret for lunch and eat on its gentle bank. This is a favourite spot of the citizens of Orléans (also called the Orléanais).

getting there

Le Rivage lies on the north bank of the Loiret at Olivet, south of central Orléans. The restaurant is sandwiched between the N20 and the A71 roads that slice through the town. Coming from the A71 motorway, take the Olivet-La Source/St-Jean-le-Blanc exit and follow the signs for Orléans-Centre. You'll turn left on to the N20 and cross the Loiret river. Be ready to turn left again soon, after the

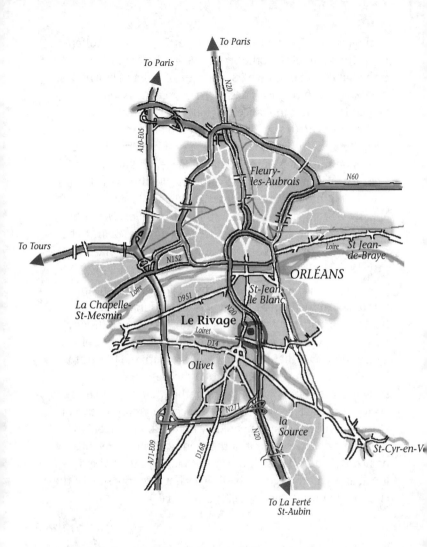

highly noticeable Auchan supermarket. Coming from central Orléans down the N20, you'll be approaching the supermarket from the opposite direction, so watch out for it and turn right at the big junction just before it.

Le Rivage

*Le Rivage, 635 rue de la Reine Blanche, 45160 Olivet, © 02 38 66 02 93,
fax 02 38 56 31 11. Closed Sun evenings Nov–Easter. Closed for holidays
28 Dec–20 Jan. Menus at 155F, 220F and 300F.*

Shaded by low, clipped trees next to the Loiret towpath, sitting indo-
lently on Le Rivage's terrace, you can look across to the gardens of the
bourgeois properties on the opposite bank, each with its little
boathouse on this calm band of river. Boats and ducks travel up and
down. People wander along the path. There are no cars to be seen,
and you can quite forget the 20th-century road culture so close by.

The car park entrance side to the restaurant is less charming than the
riverside. Le Rivage hides behind a plain front. But step onto the
bridge over the little stream to reach the entrance and you're taken
into Le Rivage's chichi heart.

Even if you're eating outside by the river, you can still catch a glimpse
of the swanky modern dining room before you reach the terrace. This
room, recently done up, has been cleverly designed with conservatory
bays that allow the light to pour in. You can look out from here onto
the terrace and river or on to the little garden. The interior is dramatic, with flourishes of flowers on pedestals. The reflective ceiling no
doubt helps to spread the light around, but it has just a soupçon of
naffness that winks ever so slightly at the mirror-on-the-bedroom-
ceiling syndrome. That may be unfair. The place has clearly been
conceived with comfort in mind.

It was the owner, Jean-Pierre Bereaud, who had the place done up.
He took over the running of the hotel in the early 1980s from
his father who started it around 50 years ago. The principal
chef, François Tassin, has been here some 20 years. The service is smart and professional, with waiters in white coats
flitting around briskly and quietly. The plates are generous,
almost to the size of ostentation. If the place shows off
slightly and some of the diners too, Le Rivage does have
all the ingredients to please. The outside terrace is very
seductive. Those well-trained trees that provide a dense covering
against the summer sun are *charmes*, by the way, hornbeam in
English. The tables are packed tight into the narrow area.

The first menu, at 155F, is certainly not bad value for four courses and gives a good taste of what the kitchen can produce. Taking this option, you only get a choice with the main course, however. This menu might start with a rich sweet entrée like a *mousse blonde de foies de volailles aux raisins blonds et Pineau des Charentes*, (chicken liver mousse with white grapes and wine) or *marbré de cuisses de canard confites et foie gras, petite salade croquante* (*confit* of duck-leg and foie gras with crisp salad). The main course will then be a choice between a fish dish or a meat dish. Even on this cheaper menu, the recipes are ornate, using special, often subtle ingredients. The slice of sturgeon comes with a warm vinaigrette flavoured with sesame oil. The chef has a fine collection of special oils and vinegars. The duck is flavoured with a balsamic vinegar and a *confiture d'oignons,* again a good choice for anyone who likes a sweet touch added to their savoury dishes. The salmon might come with a semolina flavoured with pistachio oil. After cheese, pudding might be a charlotte filled with red fruits and served with a strawberry coulis, or an aspic of red fruits in a syrup with an exotically peppery sauce.

olive oil

Your choice doesn't get much wider with the next menu up. Of the two starters we saw, the mosaic of salmon and vegetables with herby lime juice might have been unexciting to British people well used to tasting salmon, while the lamb sweetbreads might have seemed a bit too adventurous, even if served with delicious green cabbage and grilled pine kernels. The main course choice was also between the more conventional, a side of veal with fried mushrooms, and the more complex, brill in lobster sauce accompanied by artichokes in a well-seasoned vinaigrette.

You do get the full choice of puddings now, however. The *parfait glacé aux abricots et son coulis au miel de Sologne* was perfect, the cold apricot concoction melting together with the honey to leave a delicious lingering taste in the mouth. The peaches flavoured with vanilla came with a light chocolate mousse, the oranges accompanied by a coffee jelly, with ice-cream *aux senteurs de Colombie.* Or you could have opted for a minestrone of fresh fruits served with a lime and basil sorbet, or a light strawberry pastry with a salad of peppermint.

This menu might sound heavenly enough, but if you want to go one step beyond, you could go for the six-course extravagance. To give you some indication of the tone of this menu, the fish and meat dishes might be separated by a refreshing grapefruit *gratiné au Champagne*.

Le Rivage prides itself on its game in the autumn. The chef loves to prepare dishes from beasts shot in nearby Sologne. He cooks a delicious pigeon and may roast a tender rabbit expertly in rosemary. Duck features heavily too. On the top menu in the autumn were *aiguillettes de canard au vin de l'Orléanais*, a duck recipe which some might say is the finest way to use Orléanais wine in cooking.

Colvert de Sologne Rôti, Sauce Aigre-douce aux Griottes

Serves 4–6

1 prepared wild mallard or oven-ready duck, about 2.8kg/6lbs 5oz
100g/4oz butter
200g/7oz Morello cherries in unsweetened liquid, stoned
100g/4oz sugar
2 tablespoons white wine vinegar
1 litre/1 ¾ pints game stock
100ml/4fl oz sherry

Preheat the oven to 240°C/475°F (gas mark 9). Remove the giblets and clean the duck inside and out under running cold water. Pat dry. Brown the duck quickly all over by frying it in the butter over a high heat. When it is cool enough to handle, rub salt and pepper into the skin and season the inside of the duck well. Place the duck on a rack over a roasting tin and roast in the preheated oven for around 20 minutes, checking that the meat remains slightly pink, but is cooked through. Let it stand for 5 minutes or so before carving. While the duck is roasting, make the sauce. Pour the juice from the Morello cherries into a high-sided frying pan together with the sugar. Cook over a medium-high heat until the mixture has caramelised. Add the vinegar and stock. Cook, stirring, until it has reduced by about half, then add the cherries themselves. Carve the duck and arrange the pieces on warmed serving plates. At the very last minute, whisk the sherry into the sauce and spoon it over the duck.

touring around

From a distance, **Orléans** is dominated by the **Cathédral Sainte-Croix** (*open 9–12 and 2–6*) and the tiers of its towers. The rue Jeanne d'Arc was specially built to give prominence to its great 18th-century Gothic façade, neatly compartmentalized by its simple horizontal and vertical lines. Despite the monumental scale of the work, there is something delicate about it, particularly in the tracery of the windows and arches, and the tops of the two towers, which do sit rather like crowns.

Crownings there were aplenty in the Cathédrale Ste-Croix under the Capetians, but the first basilica here was built in the Dark Ages, in the 4th century. It was for this building that the hand of God appeared to spare St Euverte the trouble of consecrating the place himself. A hand blessing the church is painted on the main boss of the apse. From the 7th century the cathedral here was dedicated to the Ste-Croix, and the structure grew in size as it grew in importance. Charles le Chauve (the bald), Eudes, Robert le Pieux and Louis VI le Gros (the Fat, or perhaps one should say more elegantly, the Large) were all crowned here. The building you now see is mainly Gothic in style, but most of it was built after the traditional Gothic period had passed. Protestants in 1568 almost entirely ruined the previous construction which had taken many centuries to build. Only the radiating chapels around the choir and a couple of nave bays remained standing after one of the most monumental acts of destruction in the French Wars of Religion. In the nave, the bays were made to copy the style of the earlier ones remaining. The 19th-century windows in the side aisles to left and right as you enter the building commemorate the life of Joan of Arc, a well-known feature of the cathedral, the work of Galland and Gibelin.

The **Musée des Beaux-Arts** (*open 10–12 and 2–6; closed Tues*) lies next to the cathedral. In the centre of one of its largest rooms, a sculpture by Germain Pilon shows Monseigneur de Morvilliers, one-time bishop of Orléans, in sober-sad pose. It's as though he's dejected at all the extravagance that surrounds him. For the rest of the vast space is decorated with works from the cardinal de Richelieu's sumptuous collection, once held in his vast château in southern Touraine. On great panels by Martin Freminet, the evangelists and fathers of the Church are draped in gaudy-coloured garments and pose, vain as body-builders, self-conscious as disco-dancers. Below them, ridiculously wonderful ornate fantasies by Claude Deruet depict the elements, aristocrats at play in the scenes. Horse-drawn sleighs rushing across an icy river and snowy countryside fill the panel interpreting Water. A city alight with flames illustrates Fire. In fact, to good puritan Protestants the treasures of this museum might be regarded as a fair exhibition on the degenerate nature of the arts under France's *Ancien Régime*. This is because the greatest part of the collection is made up of 17th- and 18th-century works, when the top aristocracy and clergy were dominating the market. How could you end up anything but confused by the Counter-Reformation, going into orders and churches to find all this sensuousness spread over the walls?

After lunch you could head back into town to visit the minor Joan of Arc museums and the **Hôtel Cabu and Musée Archéologique et Historique de l'Orléanais** (*open 10–12 and 2–6; closed Tues*). The horse dedicated to the Celtic god Rudiobus poses majestically as the centrepiece in a fabulous little collection on the ground floor. The proud beast is thought to date from the 2nd century. Its dressage dignity, its flaming mane, its muscular tautness convey great power and poise. Rudiobus is sometimes compared to the Roman god of war, Mars. The wild boar, beautifully ugly brutes from the same find at Neuvy-en-Sullias, east along the Loire from Orléans, and the deer are also impressive, both deeply symbolic animals to the Celts. The great annual gathering of Gaulish druids took place somewhere east of Orléans, although the precise location remains undiscovered.

If you don't feel like braving Orléans or Joan of Arc again after lunch, you could stay in **Olivet**. Take a walk along the towpath westwards and you eventually come to a posse of charming watermills by the river. Alternatively, from in front of Le Madagascar, one of Le Rivage's restaurant neighbours to the east, you can take a boat trip down the Loiret (*check times before lunch*). You could also visit Olivet's **Parc Floral**, a very well tended public garden (*open 16 June–31 Aug, 9–7.15; April–15 June and Sept–15 Nov, 9–5.30; rest of year, 2–4.30; adm*). The Loiret source isn't particularly spectacular; the river emerges as a thick band of water straight away. The roses, irises and dahlias are the stars in this park which stretches over 35 hectares, with a butterfly greenhouse, an aviary, and innumerable flowerbeds among its attractions.

Dipping into the Sologne

La Ferme de la Lande

Thin strips of pink herringbone-patterned brick between the lines of brown beams are the recipe for some of the most picturesque Sologne architecture. Brick is *the* material of this distinct region that fills the area south of the Loire's arc through the Orléanais. In the Sologne, gone is the light limestone of the Loire. The open skies and wide valley views gradually disappear as the silver birch, oak and pine woods become thicker. Less and less agriculture takes place and heather takes over on the open lands: *lande* is the French for moorland.

La Ferme de la Lande lies just north of La Ferté-St-Aubin, which boasts a thoroughly beautiful brick château, a bit dilapidated now, but rather atmospherically so. This château served as the main setting for one of the most famous films in French cinema history, *La Règle du Jeu,* by the director Jean Renoir, son of the great Impressionist painter Auguste Renoir. One famous scene in the film takes place during a rabbit shoot in the

Sologne countryside and you could go for a walk in this countryside at the Domaine de Ciran nearby.

In the afternoon, head for the Loire west of Orléans. The Basilique de Cléry-St-André rises on the southern flood plain, the grandiose church where superstitious King Louis XI decided to be buried. Across the river on the north bank, the little riverside towns of Meung and Beaugency are beautiful and ancient, Beaugency in particular boasting several towering monuments and the oldest bridge over the Loire, patched up over the years. The wide cobbled quays show how important river trading once was in the area.

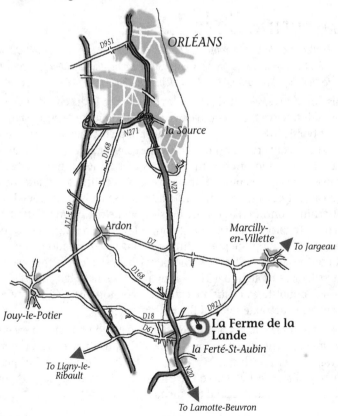

The restaurant is just north of La Ferté-St-Aubin, some 20km due south of Orléans along the N20 and close to the A71 motorway. Coming south along the N20, just before reaching La Ferté-St-Aubin, turn left (or east) on to the D921 in the direction of Marcilly-en-Villette. The longish drive down to La Ferme de la Lande is soon well indicated on the right-hand side of the road. If you're coming off the A71 motorway, from the north take the exit for Orléans-La Source just south of Orléans; if you're coming off the motorway from the south, take the exit for Lamotte-Beuvron; in each case then join the N20 to La Ferté-St-Aubin.

La Ferme de la Lande

La Ferme de la Lande, route de Marcilly, 45240 La Ferté St Aubin, ✆ 02 38 76 64 37, ✇ 02 38 64 68 87. Closed Sun evening and all day Mon; closed for holidays last fortnight in Aug. Menus at 138F, 153F, 184F and 280F.

This diminutive, secluded farm dates back to the 17th century, when it was built to serve the Château de La Ferte-St-Aubin, on whose estates it lay. It typifies the way that a fair number of pretty Sologne farmhouses have been converted into rather luxurious restaurants. Set in scatterings of pines and birches and patches of heather, a neat hedge of mauve-leafed plants protects the gravel-covered little courtyard where you can eat outside in summer. Inside, the same herring-bone brick patterning continues as on the outside, while the ceiling is beamed. An open fireplace which can heat both sides of the restaurant in colder seasons divides up the pretty dining room. The decoration may be a bit precious for some tastes, with flouncy lampshades which make the lamps look as though they're wearing floral bonnets, but the straight-backed, upholstered chairs are extremely comfortable. Old engravings of châteaux decorate some of the wall space.

There are three choices of entrées, fish, meat and pudding on each of the menus. The descriptions of the dishes are fairly elaborate-to-flowery, even pretentious. La Ferme de la Lande is the kind of place where you may feel you need the Larousse culinary dictionary by your side to help you understand the menus.

The man who keeps a keen eye on proceedings here is M. Dhellemme. Parisian by origin, he has spent all his working life in the restaurant business, starting at the bottom of the ladder as a *plongeur,* which shouldn't awaken images in your mind of a little French kitchen assistant being sent diving down into vast cauldrons to  check on the state of the sauces—it means that M. Dhellemme was once a washer-upper. Since those days he has gained experience in every aspect of the trade and worked in Berlin, Paris and Montpellier. He settled in the Sologne at the beginning of the 1990s. The chef, Laurent Poitevin, was trained here, while the delectable *pâtisseries* are prepared by the capable hands of Carlos Causte.

You might like to start with a fish entrée, for example a light *mousse-line de julienne* (ling) *à la crème de laitue.* Or there might be goat's milk putting in an early appearance as ever, but here in the form of tangy curds in a roulade of smoked sea trout. Every dish on every menu has something a little *recherché* about it. The avocado salad came with duck magret, the *hure de veau* (veal head pâté) with fresh thyme. For a symphony of whites, you could have tried the *salade de sommité de chou-fleur au blanc de volaille fumé,* the smoked white of chicken served with cauliflower heads.

The wine list is extremely extensive, with some 180 references. Why not simplify decisions immediately by sticking to a Loire Valley wine? If you're continuing with fish and seafood, you might like to opt for one of the Touraine whites. If your menus centre mainly around meats and game, try a Chinon.

Oriental touches appears in the fish menus, such as *dos de saumon sauce levant* or *papillote de julienne au poivre de Sseu-Tchouan.* Curiously we didn't come across any *sandre* on the 'basic' menus. Fear not, *sandre* aficionados, it has appeared in the past *à la carte,* served, for example, as a duo with salmon, marinated in a roulade pepped up with crab mousse, or again with duck magret smoked with star anis. A notable local fish that may surprise you on the menu is *silure de Sologne,* a very large freshwater fish that can reach up to three metres in length. It might be cooked with the sweetening touch of a Coteaux du Layon Anjou wine.

Back with the more common dishes on the main menus, duck is always a good option in the Sologne, maybe done with a classic green pepper sauce. *Génisse* liver (similar to calves' liver) is popular with the chef, who might cook it with a raspberry vinegar or with spices. The beef was accompanied by a *soubise d'oignons*, a tasty purée of onions added to a béchamel sauce.

The dish the restaurant is most proud of, however, is its *lièvre à la royale,* royal hare. This recipe recently won La Ferme de la Lande the first prize in the Journées Gastronomiques de Romorantin, a regional culinary competition. With a delicious stuffing enriched with chunks of foie gras, the hare is left to cook gently for 24 hours to absorb the flavours. It's no surprise that game should be a speciality here. The Sologne is a great hunting territory. If you're a fan, come here in autumn if you can. Another particularly interesting dish on the autumn menu was the *rôti de gigue de chevreuil et sa rosace de coings,* the roe deer offset by quince jelly, which is a speciality of St-Ay, a town on the Loire close to where we propose spending the afternoon. Quince trees still flourish in that area and their fruits are used to make the Cotignac d'Ay, a very sweet quince jelly particularly enjoyed by children in the Orléanais.

Côtes de Marcassin à la Gelée de Groseille et Suprême de Mandarines Confites

Serves 4

1–2 tablespoons oil
12 young wild boar or tender pork chops
1 small jar redcurrant jelly
8 mandarins, peeled and segmented
500ml/17fl oz game stock
40g/1½oz butter

Warm the oil in a frying pan. Fry the chops very gently in the oil for 3 minutes on each side. Remove the chops and keep them warm.

Add the redcurrant jelly to the frying pan and heat until it caramelises slightly. Add the mandarin segments, then the stock. Cook over a medium-

high heat, stirring, whisking in the butter and seasoning to taste with a
little salt and pepper, until the sauce has reduced and thickened and
become beautifully glossy (about 7–10 minutes). Meanwhile, after 4 min-
utes, remove the mandarins with a slotted spoon and arrange them round
the edges of the serving plates. Place the chops in the centre of the plates.
Spoon the sauce over the meat and serve immediately.

touring around

To appreciate something of the flora and fauna of the Sologne, visit
the **Domaine Solognot du Ciran** (*open April–Sept, 10–12 and 2–6; rest
of year, 10–12 and 2–5, but closed Tues*), by **Ménestreau-en-Villette**,
just a handful of kilometres east of La Ferté-St-Aubin along the D17.
This is one spot in this hunting-crazy region where some animals can
find temporary sanctuary. There's a quite good chance of spotting roe
deer (*chevreuils*) here, those chubby-faced, squat, white-bottomed
species. Stags and does range over much greater regions, so it is less
likely that you'll see them. However, in the fields down the slopes
from the domain, doe are reared in captivity, so you will be able to
spot a few—these ones are being prepared for pâté, but in the mean-
time they do attract the occasional stag from the wild. The woodland
is typical of the Sologne. Heather (*bruyère*) abounds. It is still locally
employed in the making of brooms, windbreaks and small decorative
objects, as it was in the past. The local word for it is *bremaille*. If you
don't see any animals on your tour, or if it's a horrible rainy day, you
can ask to watch the short nature videos kept at the domain (entries
for the Festival International du Film de la Faune Sauvage at Lamotte-
Beuvron). Some of these are absolutely wonderful.

La Ferté-St-Aubin is a typical brick-dominated little Sologne town. Its
brick **château** (*open mid-Mar–11 Nov, 10–7; rest of year, Wed, Sat, Sun
and school hols, 2–6*) is one of the most beautiful in the region. Two elegant wings, aristocratic stables and outbuildings at right angles to the
main building add to the grandiose perspective of the château seen
from the road. You can't miss it on the eastern side of the N20, north
of the town, a lovely ensemble of buildings in pale brick, with pale
yellow stone window surrounds. The entrance gate in front of the
château looks rather comical, however, two bell-hatted little *pavillons*
flanking a classical arch curiously cut into by two large grooves—

architectural purity was disfigured for the practical functioning of a drawbridge. One architectural historian has compared the behatted entrance tops to deerstalkers! Today there's a solid bridge over the water-filled moat fed by the Cosson river, which later flows past Chambord. A stone balustrade runs around the moat-protected platform. The two sections of the main *logis* were built in the 17th century. Locally, this place is known as the Château des Maréchaux. The buildings went up for the de St-Nectaire family, the older part for one Henri, the second for his son, Henri II, who became a marshal of France under Louis XIV and was known as the maréchal de La Ferté. After the Revolution, the son of the maréchal Masséna bought the place.

The tour of the château is quite eccentric, but the owner, Jacques Guyot, is good enough to point out on an explanatory board at the entrance the issues involved in restoring it. He did after all buy it once the roofs were already caving in. You can visit the two top floors unaccompanied, but the musty rooms are in a bad state of repair, those on the first floor mostly empty but for mouldy prints, those on the second floor filled with bric-a-brac. A bell rings to call you onto the guided tour of the ground floor, which takes you through some of the better preserved apartments and finishes in the basement kitchens. The guided tour fittingly starts in front of a game table. On its marble top, the killings of the day could be sorted. The 18th-century salon has been embellished with 19th-century wallpanel paintings of landscapes of the Sologne and its châteaux, which the guide can identify for you. Down below in the well-equipped basement kitchen, smoky smells and a cook dressed in white overalls greet you. After an introduction to old kitchen implements and ways, you're sat on benches to take in a very quick and simple traditional recipe. You can then taste one of the cakes that the cook has prepared earlier. The Château de La Ferté-St-Aubin turns out to be a good place for a light elevenses.

Nowadays golf is big around La Ferté-St-Aubin. But we propose an afternoon pursuing more traditional Loire tourist activities. From a little north of the town, take the D18 northwestwards for the Basilique de Cléry-St-André. From many angles on the southern valley plain this church stands out like a great vessel in a desert—there are just a few trees scattered here and there. It's thanks to a large dose of medieval superstition that diminutive Cléry-St-André was donated a disproportionately vast church looming over the village. In 1280 a local farmer ploughing his field is said to have dug up a statue of a woman and child. They turned out to be the Virgin and baby Jesus, of course, and began to work miracles. Such was the impact that royal Capetian patronage was quickly in on the act. Philippe IV le Bel's generous sponsorship allowed for the building of a splendid church and it became an important stop on the pilgrimage route from Paris to St James of Compostela. The English army passing this way in the second half of the Hundred Years War showed absolutely no respect for the holy mother and child or their achievements and destroyed Philippe le Bel's church. Miracle of miracles, the Virgin and child survived, however. They still grace the church, perched high up in an over-elaborate 19th-century neo-Byzantine structure. The brown-robed Mary (apparently 12th century, the experts say, given the peculiar way she lifts the child in front of her) looks distinctly surprised by all these events, all this attention and the elevation. Her previous home destroyed, building got under way for a new church to house her. The count of Dunois, aided by King Charles VII, supported the beginning of the works. Yellower Cher limestone was selected to replace the greyer Beauce limestone of the earlier church. But progress on the building was slow until Louis XI spurred on the work as a consequence of what he interpreted as an act of divine intervention.

As the *dauphin*, or heir to the French throne, in 1443 Louis had been fighting the English up in Dieppe with the count of Dunois. The battle was going against the French. The story has it that Louis asked Dunois in which direction he should look to the Virgin of Cléry. Instructed, Louis prayed to her for help. She apparently interceded, not only extricating the French from a sticky situation, but also reversing the tide, bringing them victory. In repayment of the Virgin's largesse, Louis became personally involved in the rebuilding of her church at Cléry-St-André and showered money on the project. Most significantly, the king of superstition decided to be buried here. So anxious was he to see the place built before his death that he even spent a couple of months at Cléry-St-André in 1482 as the site was nearing completion and his health failing. But the church was not quite ready by the time he passed away in 1483. His skull, a tomb effigy and the royal paranoiac's peephole from his private room count among the church's curiosities.

A patched-up, bumpy medieval bridge, cobbled quays, vast plane trees shielding the low waterfront houses, and behind them soaring medieval monuments... Seen from the south side of its bumbling old bridge, the oldest one on the Loire, **Beaugency** is one of the most beautiful towns along the river. Up the hill lies a surprising number of interesting houses and monuments packed close together within the town ramparts. The most imposing evidence of Beaugency's medieval importance is the massive keep, known as the tour de César. There are a couple of other keeps like this along the Loire, for example at Loches, which show the formidable nature of this type of early feudal military architecture. This one dates from the last quarter of the 11th century and still retains its towering severity (some 36m of it), this despite the beautiful colour of the material in which it is built, the newer mullion windows added in the 16th century, and its abandoned air, with plants growing in places up the walls and crows now lords of the manor. It isn't possible to visit the tower, such is its state of disrepair.

The church of Notre-Dame next to the keep originates from the same period, but, like it, was badly damaged by religious fire in 1567, then restored in 1642. This is the church which saw the annulment of Eleanor of Aquitaine's marriage to Louis VII. She was remarried soon after to Henri Plantaganêt of Anjou down the Loire, who became King Henry II of England in 1154. The church still has a Romanesque feel within. Massive Romanesque columns hold up the nave and aisles, with bold capital designs, some with primitive foliage, others with fighting or humorous figures. One shows a comically naïve stylized bird; on another, the top of the capital has been cleverly exploited to form a man's magnificently large nose! You can walk round the lovely open ambulatory at the choir end and back up to the organ at the entrance with finely carved wood panels in front.

Beaugency's absurdly overdecorated town hall (*open 10–12 and 2–5 except Sat pm, Sun and public hols*) houses eight exquisitely executed embroideries you might care to take a look at, their original provenance and precise symbolism a mystery.

The Forests Around Chambord that Teem with Châteaux

If you're on a holiday visiting innumerable châteaux it seems only fair that you should stop and lunch in the odd one rather than always being turfed out at midday. The edge of the Sologne forest southeast of Blois positively teems with châteaux open to tourists. And there is one at which you can eat which shouldn't be missed. It's the Château du Breuil, near Cour-Cheverny and Cheverny.

You could sandwich your lunch at the Château du Breuil between two giant slabs of Loire châteaux by visiting the Château de Chambord, the most preposterously outsized of 'hunting lodges', in the morning and the Château de Cheverny, considered by many to be the most sophisticated of the region's châteaux, in the afternoon. These two count among the most famous châteaux not just in the Loire Valley, but in the whole of France.

Le Château du Breuil

If you want to avoid the crowds that flock to these two châteaux, try to arrive as close as possible to opening hours. Or head for one of the handful of lesser-known châteaux so close

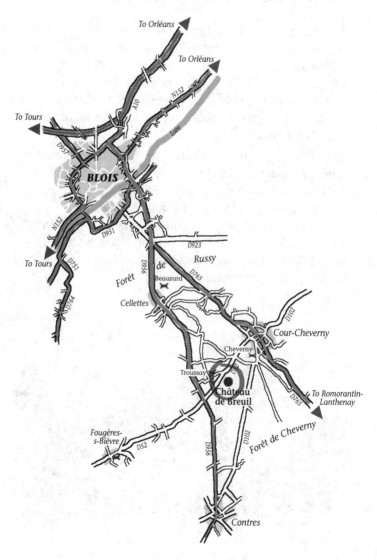

to the Château du Breuil. Troussay, the nearest, is strictly speaking a *gentilhommière*, a country manor for a nobleman a step down from a lord. The Château de Villesavin is charmingly discreet and hidden in contrast to Chambord's hulking presence.

The Château du Breuil is also situated in wine country, in the midst of the AOC Cour-Cheverny. You could always be bold, and drop one of your tourist engagements with a château to go on a wine-tasting instead.

getting there

The Château du Breuil lies close to the D765 connecting Blois with Romorantin-Lanthenay. Coming from the A10 motorway, take the Blois exit and head south of the Loire for Romorantin. Turn off the D765 at Cour-Cheverny, maybe taking a glimpse at the Château de Cheverny from the gates at the end of its park as an appetizer. The Château du Breuil lies off the D52 going to Fougères-sur-Bièvre.

Château du Breuil

Château du Breuil, route de Fougères-sur-Bièvre (D52), 41700 Cheverny,
℡ 02 54 44 20 20, ✆ 02 54 44 30 40. Closed Sun eve and all Mon out of
season. In season, closed just Mony lunchtime. Closed for holidays 15
Nov–15 Feb. Menus 195F, 250F and 375F.

A magical driveway through dense woods, so deeply leafy in summer that even the strongest of sunbeams finds it hard to cut through, leads to the clearing in which the Château du Breuil stands. M. Têtenoire and his wife, who run the property with discreet care, bought this château in 1988. M. Têtenoire is actually Parisian by birth, but from the age of seven came on holidays to a family home in the Val de Loire. Working in the Loire Valley since 1977, the couple long held the dream of running a château of their own as a hotel and restaurant. They opened their château's doors in 1989.

The château is of 18th-century origin, but parts of it burned down in the 1820s and were rebuilt. It is therefore not the archetypal Loire Renaissance château owned by a courtier or a king, more a château typical of the wealthy across France in the last century. And its façades are roughcast rather than of cut stone, except around the edges. All is calm in the Château du Breuil's clearing, the atmosphere elegant. You feel far from the madding crowds of the major tourist châteaux now. The Têtenoires don't insist on a strict dress code in their château, but you'll probably feel a little embarrassed by the setting if you turn up in shorts, while sandals and socks would be an insult to the décor.

Start with an apéritif in the *salon double*. This is a splendid room, light and spacious, furnished mainly in Louis XVI style. The walls are covered with wood panelling in shades of blue and carved with details of flowers. The plaster work on the ceiling carries on with further ornate flower patterns and swirls. On the marble fireplace stand a lavish golden clock and candelabra, on another fireplace, delightful golden peasants! A very old and elegant piano encased in wood stands open ready for someone to play it. Parquet flooring, chairs embroidered with roses, big lampshades and tall draped curtains contribute to the splendid *salon* atmosphere. The windows give onto the park. An oak lords it over the lawn, but many of the plants in the garden are less sturdy, regularly ravaged by roe deer. You might try a really unusual but very local wine as an apéritif here, a Crémant de Cheverny produced by Christian Tessier. This sparkling wine has won a gold medal at a competition in Paris for one vintage, which is a respectable achievement.

The dining room is in Directoire style, neoclassical late 18th century, with fan chairs and lots of dark wood. This is lightened by yellow walls above the band of wood panelling. Silver wine buckets stand to attention by the tables. The chef at the Château du Breuil, Patrick Léonce, is actually from Provence, and the influence of his native region shows through in the cuisine. One excellent menu, the 'Clin d'Œil Provençal' pays more than passing recognition to the culinary traditions of southeast France. The chef's cooking can range from superlative to fabulous and is extremely refined.

The *clin d'œil provençal* is actually the cheapest menu, but offers a fine four courses. For the entrée you might have a choice between pressed ricotta and *pommes d'amour confites*—*pomme d'amour* is the Provençal euphemism for a tomato—served with croûtons spread with *foie blond* and a salad of marinaded anchovies accompanied by bread covered with tomatoes. For the main course on this menu when we visited, the choice was between angler fish baked in bacon and served with vegetable-stuffed squid, and rabbit with horseradish 'spaghetti', a skewer of liver, and a light sauce flavoured with thyme. Here is a chef who knows how to look for interesting combinations of tastes. The cheese-board presents a healthy selection from across France, not just the Loire or Provence. For the puddings the chef likes to concentrate on fresh fruits in summer. Many of the desserts, like the basket of summer fruits with a lemon *crème glacée* (a proper, rich, definitely superior ice-cream), revolve around these. He prepares very refreshing sorbets. There should always be an elaborate chocolate option, of course, like the absorbing *macaron moelleux et fondant au cacao au croustillant d'amande* (a creamy, chewy chocolate and almond macaroon concoction), a serious pudding to get your teeth into.

Another menu, '*Entre Mer et Sologne*', revealed yet more Provençal tendencies, the main dish of *lasagne de sanglier aux pieds de cochon* (lasagne of boar with trotters) served with a *ragoût de légumes au pistou*, the latter a Provençal basil paste. It must be added, however, that at the Château du Breuil we tasted the best *sandre* recipe we have experienced to date along the Loire.

In season some of the vegetables and fruit are grown locally. The asparagus come from around here, the strawberries and raspberries from a little local producer. The young pigeon too is reared close by and in autumn the game and the mushrooms are easily supplied from the Sologne forest. We suppose, given the Têtenoires' vendetta against the ravaging deer, that it wouldn't be surprising if the venison were very local indeed.

If you're sticking with fish and seafood as a main course, M. Têtenoire might recommend a Christian Tessier Cheverny Blanc, made from a mix of Chardonnay and Sauvignon, with plenty of bouquet and a very fruity flavour. For certain meat dishes he might also recommend a local Cheverny or Cour-Cheverny Rouge, or even a Sancerre Rouge. He is the kind of man from whom it's worth asking advice, as he'll give you sensible, unfussy recommendations.

Sandre Rôti sur la Peau, Jus Parfumé aux Zestes

Serves 4

4 thick fillets of pikeperch or mackerel, each about 135g/14¾ oz
1 lemon
4 heads chicory
1–2 tablespoons duck fat or dripping
1 orange
300ml/½ pint chicken stock

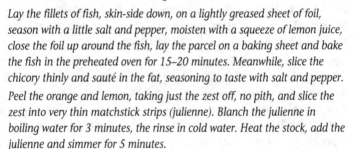

Preheat the oven to 180°C/350°F (gas mark 4)

Lay the fillets of fish, skin-side down, on a lightly greased sheet of foil, season with a little salt and pepper, moisten with a squeeze of lemon juice, close the foil up around the fish, lay the parcel on a baking sheet and bake the fish in the preheated oven for 15–20 minutes. Meanwhile, slice the chicory thinly and sauté in the fat, seasoning to taste with salt and pepper.

Peel the orange and lemon, taking just the zest off, no pith, and slice the zest into very thin matchstick strips (julienne). Blanch the julienne in boiling water for 3 minutes, the rinse in cold water. Heat the stock, add the julienne and simmer for 5 minutes.

To serve, place some chicory in the centre of each plate, a fillet of fish on the chicory and pour some sauce over the top.

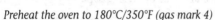

touring around

From whichever way you approach the **Château de Chambord** (*open July and Aug, 9.30–5.45; 2 Nov–June, 9.30–11.45 and 2–4.45; Sept–Oct, 9.30–11.45 and 2–5.45; château closes 45 mins after last time stated*) through the long alleys of the mysterious walled forest that encircles it, it makes a staggering sight. On first seeing it you immediately realize you're in front of one of the great buildings of the world. Chambord is a palace, rather than the traditional cottage, in a glade.

'If the main idea was to build a hunting pavilion, then Chambord was a failure!' one guide to the Château de Chambord once said jokingly to us. Chambord also exposes the weakness of a vain king yielding to voracious, monstrous greed. The competition was fierce. François I came to the throne when the young King Henry VIII ruled England and soon after Charles of Hapsburg would outbid them both—with the massive financial backing of the German banker Jacob Fugger—in the stakes to become Holy Roman Emperor.

The long, regular expanses of Chambord's walls rise to roofs whose plethora of extravagantly decorated forms make the place look like a riotously exuberant self-contained royal city...or, such is the density of turrets, lanterns, chimneys and *lucarnes*, like several châteaux squashed into one. In fact, Chambord stands out from other royal Loire châteaux precisely because it was not built as an amalgamation of architectural projects of different periods, but comes from a coherent, new, carefully planned project.

Building work began on Chambord in 1519. The central structure, while keeping the imposing corner towers of French medieval architecture, is on a ground-breaking Greek-cross plan, with at its core an extraordinary double spiral staircase crowned by the fleur de lys, symbol of French royalty. François I had called over Leonardo da Vinci to serve him in the Loire, and the Florentine genius's name is associated with the place, although the part that the Italian Domenico da Cortona played is more certain. The vast enterprise was well on the way to completion when François I died in 1547.

Someone has calculated that the château, in its 470 or so years of existence, has only been lived in for 20 years. 'This history of inoccupation shows what a failed real estate venture Chambord was', the guides explain, finding a telling modern idiom. A white elephant if ever there was one. All these apartments which have virtually never been occupied... Chambord was an exercise in sheer wasteful royal extravagance, utterly impractical, vastly preposterous. What were you to do with so many apartments? An answer lies in Versailles, of course. Louis XIV was virtually the only proprietor to have found Chambord to his size, just right for a little hunting jaunt in the country.

The mammoth structure stands pretty empty nowadays, although a museum on hunting takes up a small number of the many hundreds of rooms. The double staircase and the roofscapes make for the most enjoyable part of a visit, unless you try to get on one of the special architectural tours. Chambord was moated for centuries, but the ditch was filled in. However, just recently, boating has begun on the river

Cosson which passes through Chambord's glade, so you could take to the water to enjoy the unforgettable views of the château from there.

If you already know Chambord, or want to avoid crowds, try visiting the **Château de Villesavin** a short way south (*open Mar–Sept, 10–12 and 2–7; Oct–20 Dec, 2–5; closed Jan–Feb*). A chip off the old block of Chambord is the way Villesavin is frequently described—or at least a little piece of the monster's roof that might have miraculously blown off in the wind and landed in the middle of these charming woods, close to the little Beuvron river. Some say that it was no miracle, but that the man for whom Villesavin was built, Jean Le Breton, diverted funds and workers from the king's building site to construct himself a nice little château on the side. The guide humorously describes this place as the *'cabane de chantier de Chambord* (the builders' hut for Chambord's building site)'. The construction of Villesavin began at the end of 1526 or beginning of 1527 and was completed within ten years.

The main courtyard with its splendid Renaissance fountain and typical Loire *lucarnes* is full of charm. You can visit the tiny chapel with badly worn but interested frescoes, the dovecote, and several rooms inside, including a couple of atmospheric old kitchens.

The **Château de Cheverny** (*open June–15 Sept, 9.15–6.45; rest of the year, 9.30–12 and 2.15–5*) is the most refined Loire château, a lesson in French taste. A generous smooth lawn leads to the immaculate front. This main façade is so white and clean and the stones laid in such a seamless manner that many have mistaken the effect for whitewashed clapboard. Some might feel it a weakness that an expensive cut-stone façade should be cheapened by a deceptive resemblance to a less noble material. This is, however, a great piece of Loire architecture, but a quite rare phenomenon, being blatantly 17th-century. Jacques Bougier, or Boyer of Blois as he was also known, was the architect. He planned this work for Henri Hurault, one-time governor of the town, for whom any vestige of the previous château on the site was wiped away.

Cheverny isn't a vast château, but slim and elegant, so there aren't endless rooms to be seen inside. It is sumptuously furnished, though. The tour takes you round much of the ground and first floors. You enter via the central pavilion housing the staircase. Cheverny is the Loire château which probably boasts the finest collection of paintings.

The place resembles a fine arts gallery in this respect, but it is also a château still clearly lived in and very lovingly maintained.

The outstanding feature of the interiors is the wall paintings by Jean Mosnier, well restored in the 19th century. Mosnier's work dates from the origins of the château and is particularly splendid in the anachronistically named *salle des gardes*. Even the wainscot is decorated with allegorical interpretations of classical epigrams. The period's attachment to the classical pervades all Mosnier's work, the painting above the fireplace depicting the death of Adonis. Many of the pictures are actually incorporated into the panelling. Golds and blues dominate the scheme, but arrays of bright flowers add further colour. The long gallery contains some earlier, freestanding family portraits, including three by the superlative French court painter of the mid-16th century, François Clouet. Still greater portraits look down on you from the drawing room. Jeanne d'Aragon may have been painted in Raphael's studio around 1515. The Titian portrait shows the young Cosimo de' Medici. The Italian influence has turned Mannerist here. Grotesque gilded caryatids prop up the monumental fireplaces. On the first floor, the so-called *chambre du roi* is gilded with more dazzling painting by Mosnier, putti floating on gold.

The park in which the château stands is elegant too, with its spacious well-kempt lawns. It's best known for its pack of hunt dogs which are to be seen chasing across the lawn in most clichéd photographs of the place. Ordinarily you can go and watch the miserable mutts lazing around in their cages. Feeding time is at 5pm in high season.

Again, if you've already visited Cheverny in the past or are looking for a more peaceful tour, try **Troussay** (*open June–Aug, 10–7; Sept, 10–1 and 2–6; French school hols at Easter and All Saints', 10.30–12.30 and 2–6; other periods between Easter and All Saints', Sun and public hols, 10.30–12.30 and 2–6*). Troussay is a *gentilhommière* or manor house rather than a château. It provides a good example of the architecture and living arrangements of the minor nobility. But its comparatively modest frame contains some rather grand pieces of decorative art taken from other, larger Loire châteaux and houses that fell into disrepair. If you prefer to visit one of the local winemakers, ask M. Têtenoire for directions to Christian Tessier's Domaine de la Desoucherie (✆ *02 54 79 90 08;* ✆ *02 54 79 22 48*).

Eating with Herons on the Loire near Blois

The first time I went to the Château de Beauregard a stag was waiting to greet me in the long wood-lined drive. It was about 9am and the morning traffic was rushing along the D765 to Blois not 500 metres away. Once you reach it, the Château de Beauregard isn't the most spectacular of châteaux from the outside, but it conceals a couple of remarkable rooms within. Outside in the grounds, the château has recently created an ornamental garden, the *jardin des portraits,* that in some way imitates the boxes of the painted panels.

The dramatically sited and highly picturesque Loire château that is best known to French gardeners, however, is the Château de Chaumont-sur-Loire, host to the annual Festival International du Jardin. Chaumont lies a little west of Beauregard along the south bank of the Loire, overlooking the river majestically from its hillside. Owned for a period by Queen Catherine de' Medici, once her husband Henri II died, she swapped it for his favoured mistress Diane de Poitiers's Château de Chenonceau on the Cher. Legend has it that

Le Château de Blois

Chaumont is where Catherine de' Medici's astrologer conjured up in the queen's mirror a cruel vision of the fate of her sons' short reigns and the end of the Valois dynasty.

You can cross the Loire at Chaumont to follow the north bank eastwards to the restaurant L'Espérance. It lies just outside Blois, the city where you can spend a healthy afternoon traipsing up and down its hills and through the corridors and museums of its vast château. Once the home of a famous chivalric poet-duke, Charles d'Orléans, a 15th-century nobleman who inspired Joan of Arc, it became the château of a king when Charles's son Louis inherited the French throne by an accident. Blois became, briefly, the capital of the kingdom and courtiers built splendid homes on its hillsides.

getting there

From the centre of Blois, go westwards in the direction of Tours, keeping to the north bank of the Loire. Once on the quai Ulysse Besnard, slow down to look out for the restaurant, on the right-hand side. Given its architecture, it's not that hard to spot. With its comical columns, it looks more like an Italian house that's got away with avoiding planning permission than a typical Loire-side home. Some trellises attempt to hide its rather ugly lower wall. You can park off the road in front of them relatively easily.

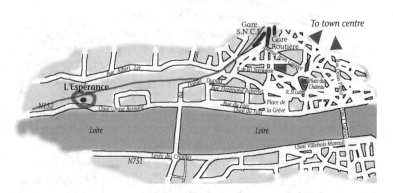

L'Espérance

L'Espérance, 189 quai Ulysse Besnard, 41000 Blois, ☎ 02 54 78 09 01,
✉ 02 54 56 17 86. Closed Sun pm and Mon. Closed for a fortnight in
mid-Aug and for French Feb school hols. Menus at 130F, 175F, 245F.

OK, so L'Espérance may look like a planning fiasco from the outside
and it does lie next to the busy Loire-side road connecting Blois with
Tours, but seeing it in those terms doesn't do justice to the restaurant.
Climb up to the entrance and then take a seat in the lower, front
dining room (ask for *une table avec une belle vue sur la Loire* when you
book). You're then perched high above the road, looking down onto
the river and the flat bank opposite.

L'Espérance has that rare advantage in terms of Loire restaurants of
looking so directly onto the great river. The view isn't quite perfect as
you can't help noticing the electricity lines and pylons insensitively
sited on the other bank. But on the summer day we ate there, with the
river low enough to reveal its characteristic sand banks in places,
during the meal we saw up to five herons at one time. On other days
you may see cormorants fishing.

The décor inside the restaurant isn't particularly exciting, with grey
carpet, simple black chairs and flowery curtains, but the decoration on
the plates more than makes up for a slightly ordinary look. There are
only around ten tables in the lower dining room giving directly onto
the Loire, so do make sure you book one of those. The connecting
upper dining room isn't so well placed.

With its view of the river it isn't entirely surprising
that L'Espérance has made fish its forte. Seafood
too features strongly. And the crayfish may even
be local sometimes. Raphaël Guillot is the chef,
while Chantal his wife looks after the service.
They have been here since the late 1980s. The *menu
du marché* at 130F varies each day, but the main menu
is the *menu gourmet,* a satisfying four courses. If you feel like both fish
and meat, the five-course menu comes at 245F.

A popular starter is the *salade folle espérance,* warm langoustines mixed
with thin slices of foie gras. Anyone who has licked their fingers after
eating langoustines cooked in butter will know what a pleasure that

can be, so perhaps you can imagine what langoustines taste like with a little foie gras melting over them. Or how about a mix of skate and salmon in a cucumber jelly, served with fried chanterelle mushrooms flavoured with lemon juice? Or thin stripes of salmon served with oyster fritters? There will also be a meat choice among the starters, such as the melon slices with lamb ham smoked by the restaurant—smoked lamb is a surprisingly tasty preparation well worth trying.

Among the main fish dishes, sea fish dominates. One of the best mixes we sampled was the sea bream and breaded *coquilles St-Jacques* with pistachios. Or for something more daring, you could try the skate stuffed with green cabbage and served with slices of grilled *andouillette,* chitterling sausage. Among the lake fish that have appeared at L'Espérance recently, *omble chevalier* is the strange sounding char, usually associated with Lake Annecy in eastern France, very close to Switzerland. The Guillots actually lived in Geneva for a time. The char came *en croûte,* in pastry, covered with sesame seeds and artichokes, a vegetable Catherine de' Medici is supposed to have introduced to France. Or there may be our favourite *sandre,* received fresh, cooked for example in olive and tarragon oil, or even served with those local crayfish.

Some of the meat dishes came with shellfish too. Crayfish have featured in the recent past both with tender pork in tarragon and with suprême of young chicken. The *crépine de lapereau* is a sausage filled with rabbit and hazlenuts, with gambas flambéd in whisky added as well as the fresh foie gras! Luxurious enough for you? The lamb cutlets came with a grated goat's cheese topping accompanied by celeriac and walnuts. The vegetables were excellent all round. The potatoes were presented as a millefeuille, the mixed vegetables in a little parcel of pastry known as an *aumonière,* apparently after its similarity to the purse that pilgrims used to carry on their journeys.

On to the excellent puddings. Here, as in some of the main dishes, you may spot the odd Provençal touch, for example with the *sabayon de fruits de saison aux odeurs de lavande et Champagne, blanc manger aux amandes* (fruit sabayon flavoured with lavender and champagne), or in the crackly millefeuille with orgeat and warmed mangoes flavoured with lavender. If you find *crème brûlée* a bit rich by itself, a good way to appreciate it is the way it's served here, herb-flavoured and served with a *brochette de fruits*, an accompanying refreshing skewer of fresh fruit.

You used to be able to visit the Poulain chocolate factory in Blois. Poulain is a household name in France, with its symbol of a foal. After Cadbury's bought the Blésois company, visits were stopped. But M. Guillot has continued to champion the chocolate. Loire pears and chocolate go very well together, so the sweet-toothed among you might be delighted by the *poire farcie au chocolat chaud et panée à la pistache, îles flottantes caramelisées*. The best chocolate pudding to try, though, would be the *assiette du chocolatier*, which actually gives you the opportunity of sampling several cocoa desserts on the one plate.

Charlotte d'Asperges au Crabe, Sucette de Volaille au Jus Réduit

Serves 4

1kg/2lbs 4oz white asparagus spears
handful green asparagus spears
2 eggs
100ml/4fl oz vinaigrette made from equal parts walnut oil and shallot
    vinegar
100 ml/4fl oz mayonnaise
12 chicken manchons (meat from the upper part of the wing)
100ml/4fl oz chicken stock
handful fresh chives
100ml/4fl oz single cream
2 tomatoes
250g/9oz mixed salad leaves, washed, trimmed and shredded
250g/9oz cooked mixed crabmeat and claws
salt and pepper

Preheat the oven to 180°C/350°F (gas mark 4).

Cook the asparagus in boiling salted water until just tender. Rinse under cold running water, and cut into 3–4cm/1¼–1½in lengths and set to one side. Hard-boil the eggs. Separate the whites from the yolks, cut up the egg whites and mix them with the vinaigrette. Mix the yolks with the mayonnaise. Bone the chicken manchons, lay them on a lightly greased baking sheet and cook them in the preheated oven for 15 mins. Meanwhile, heat the stock in a saucepan and leave it to reduce by half. Add the manchons and set aside. While the stock is reducing, chop the chives finely. Add the chives to the cream and season to taste with salt and pepper. To peel the tomatoes, cut a cross in the skin on the bottom of each tomato, plunge into boiling water for about 30 seconds, then into cold water. The skins will now come off easily. Cut the tomatoes into quarters, scoop out the seeds, then dice the flesh. Season to taste with salt and pepper.

Now you can construct the charlotte. Arrange the asparagus pieces around the edges of a charlotte mould. Then put the salad in a layer in the bottom of the mould, followed by a layer of the egg yolk mayonnaise, then the egg whites in vinaigrette, then the tomatoes. Lay the crabmeat on top of the egg whites. Finally, add a layer of the cream and chives mixture. Place the manchons here and there, pour the stock over, and decorate the charlotte with the crab claws.

touring around

The sober, if not dull exterior of the **Château de Beauregard** (*open July and Aug, 9.30–6.30; Apr–Sept, 9.30–12 and 2–6.30; Oct–mid-Jan and mid-Feb–Mar—during which periods closed Wed—9.30–12 and 2–5*) gives no clue to the rank upon rank of portraits of the famous that await you inside. This is a château of what is termed the second French Renaissance, from around the middle of the 16th century. Classical order is being imposed and any lingering playful influences of Gothic have been wiped out. The château's 17th-century Galerie des Illustres, the splendid highlight of the tour, offers a majestic lesson in history, as well as in the looks and fashions of some of the supreme figures across centuries of western European history. The place is unique along the Loire, but not in France, and there was in fact something of a vogue in the 17th century for such galleries. The Italian Paulo Jove is credited with launching the fashion in his villa near Lake Como in the 16th century. Beauregard has a staggering 327 portraits, packed close together, 'like sheets of postage stamps' as a guide neatly reduces it. A book of *Eloges*, or eulogies, accompanied the château's paintings. The guides here can give you a head-spinning lesson on the major figures in the Hundred Years War and the French Wars of Religion. Americans might like to look out for the Florentine explorer Amerigo Vespucci in particular.

The **Château de Chaumont** (*open 15 Mar–Sept, 9.30–6; Oct–14 Mar, 10–4.30—the château closes 30 mins after last times indicated; closed 1 Jan, 1 May, 1 and 11 Nov and 25 Dec; the park closes at nightfall*) looks dramatically down on to the Loire, one of the best-situated of all the river's châteaux. 'Hot mount' appears at first glance to be the trendy translation for 'Chaumont', but it actually derives from the Latin for bald mound. Sturdy, white and seductively aloof on its now wooded hillside, the château's elevated position means there's quite a climb up the ramp to it. Building began early in the 1470s after the previous castle had been destroyed on Louis XI's orders as punishment for Pierre d'Amboise's part in the rebellion of the *Ligue du Bien Public*. But Pierre had subsequently been pardoned and allowed to construct a new château on the spot. He had the north and west wings built before his death in 1473. His grandson Charles II d'Amboise inherited Chaumont in 1481. It was only from 1498 to 1510, a vital period in the change in French style, that the rest of the château was completed.

Around the middle of the 18th century, Jacques-Donatien Le Ray bought Chaumont and turned it into a centre of artistic production from the 1770s. The English glass painter Robert Scott Godfrey came, as did the Italian potter J.B. Nini, among whose terracotta medallions one represents a famous American visitor and ambassador of the time, Benjamin Franklin. This period of artistic activity was followed by one of abandonment at the start of the 19th century. But wealthy new owners came to the rescue. The interior bears the marks of 19th-century good living, with underfloor heating added along with the collection of fine art pillaged from a pot-pourri of places.

If you visit Chaumont in the summer months, go to the Festival International des Jardins (*open 15 June–20 October, 9–nightfall*) rather than into the château. Modern garden designers are given the chance to create compact contemporary experimental models. You reach the festival displays via bridges over a miniature ravine and, in one place, a staircase placed in the trunk of a massive old tree. These are not aristocratic gardens being presented, but manageable suburban-sized plots, extremely imaginatively designed and planted. The cutting edge of gardening is on show: many displays are conceptual, even political, although the 1996 event went by the charming title of *30 jardins 'poétiquement corrects'*!

Having known the **Château de Blois** (*open every day except 1 Jan and 25 Dec; 15 June–Aug, 9–7.15; mid-Mar–mid-Jun and Sept–mid-Oct, 9–5.45; mid-Oct–mid-Mar, 9–11.45 and 2–4.45*) as a dirt-blackened, miserable wretch, a picture of grandeur aged and abandoned, its transformation in the last 10 years is quite staggering. It's like an old, wrinkled movie star worn by time who's finally decided to have the facelifts...but they've worked pretty well, the rejuvenating effects clearly and happily visible. Within, the series of museums have all been very recently revised or reinvented. The place now houses: an archaeological museum; a *musée lapidaire*, or museum of old stones; furniture and furnishings collections in the François I wing; and Blois's fine arts museum. All these elements combine to make this one of the richest buildings in provincial France.

The mismatched wings of the château are like an architectural game of Misfits, pieces of four clashing styles shoved next to each other. The effect is by no means unattractive, and even rather amusing. Each piece is a magnificent example of its own style. The Louis XII outer façade by which you enter is late Gothic in temperament, not Renaissance, although it was begun in 1499. Symmetry was not a major consideration; even the entrance gateway lies off centre. The windows, while spacious and showing the greater openness of late Gothic, were decorated with the typical exuberant motifs of that period and topped by characteristic Loire *lucarnes*. The trellis patterning in brick, with only trimmings in stone, follows the architectural fashion of the time. But there are notable elements of French Gothic missing here; no sturdy corner towers, no battlements, no fortified gateway, no drawbridge. A monkey playing the bagpipes is just one of the typical late Gothic sculptures high up on the inner Louis XII façade.

The François I wing's courtyard façade is a lavish display of the Gothic fusing with the Renaissance. It was begun in 1515, almost immediately after François, who had married Louis XII's daughter Claude, had inherited the throne. Symmetry is still not especially sought, but a grid of horizontal lines, an Italian influence, breaks the traditional vertical movement of French Gothic. The high-relief salamanders plastered over the walls may present a Gothic emblematic display, but the details in the wealth of other decoration are very much Italianate.

The Gaston d'Orléans wing stands in stark, ordered contrast to the delightfully eccentric, slightly chaotic other wings. Symmetry and the classical orders triumph in the bright light grey stone of Mansart's work. Gone are the joyously individualistic elements of Gothic decoration. Gone are the elevating exuberant *lucarnes* which stretch the gaze skywards. There is classical playfulness to Mansart's design, but here the joviality comes in the subtle use of the double pilaster and other such humorous classical copybook elements.

Go for a wander through the interiors of the various wings. In the François I wing look out for Félix Dubois' flowery 19th-century decoration, the stained glass from the same period in the Oratory, and the ornate Cabinet de Travail, its carved wood panelling like a copybook of Renaissance decorative motifs. This wing also witnessed one of the most infamous assassinations in French history. The beleaguered King Henri III had the overbearing leader of the ultra-Catholic *Ligue* in the Wars of Religion, Henri, duc de Guise, killed in his royal chambers.

After passing through the 13th-century great medieval hall, visit the Musée des Beaux-Arts in the Louis XII wing. The collection doesn't stem from the patronage of kings and princes, but consists mainly of donations from wealthy Blésois of the 19th century. The most interesting room in historical terms, the salle des Guises, relates in pictures the story of the Blois assassination and Henri III's own demise. He is shown taking the last royal Valois gasp..

If you're looking for a place to eat in Blois in the evening, try Au Rendez-Vous des Pêcheurs, 27 rue du Foix, ✆ 02 54 74 67 48, ✆ 02 54 74 47 67 (*menu at 140F; closed Sun, Mon lunchtime, public hols, Feb school hols and, please note, 1–22 Aug*). This little town house, down close by the forbiddingly spiky-towered Eglise St-Nicolas, was formerly a grocer's shop, now crammed, even slightly cramped, with good things. The food is refined, with fish and seafood a particular speciality. For more regal surroundings you could eat in the Orangerie du Château, 1 avenue Jean Laigret, behind the castle, ✆ 02 54 78 05 36, fax 02 54 78 22 78 (*menus 120–320F; closed Mon, and Sun evening out of season*). It faces the dramatic loggiaed façade of the François I wing.

An Old Inn and Napoleonic Empire in the Berry

Sancerre is in northeastern Berry, Valençay in northwestern Berry, Sancerre in the *département* of the Cher, Valençay in the *département* of the Indre—these two *départements* constitute the modern equivalent of the Ancien Régime French province of Berry. The Valençay area produces both wine and goat's cheese like the Sancerrois, but its cheese is much better known than its wine. It often takes the curious form of a decapitated pyramid. The story goes that Napoleon's great minister Talleyrand, wishing to put an end to bad memories of Napoleon's disastrous Egyptian campaign, sliced off the cheese's top with his sabre and the trend caught on!

Talleyrand is the malicious genius whose memory most haunts the great Château de Valençay. Talleyrand was given the place by Napoleon to entertain foreign dignitaries with whom the emperor was pleased. And the captured Spanish royal family was kept on château-arrest here for some time. But the château with its great distinctive pepper-pot towers dates in good part back to the 16th century.

l'Auberge St Fiacre

After lunch at Veuil, a village down the charming little Nahon valley from Valençay, you could head on to another of the Berry's finest châteaux, the jewel box of Bouges. A neat rectangle of a building, this doll's house château retains fine furnishings throughout. The rooms are often full of flowers from the eccentric walled garden, while the landscaped grounds make for an idyllic afternoon walk.

The Berry is much, much quieter than the Loire Valley and even Valençay, with the attraction of a château that still counts in touristic terms as one of the dozen most interesting of the Loire, can be very quiet outside the main tourist season.

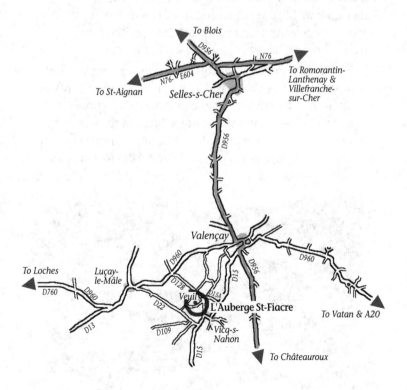

Veuil is 7km southwest of Valençay. Valençay isn't far from the A20 motorway—take the Vatan exit and follow the D960. If you're approaching Valençay from the Cher valley, drop south at Selles-sur-Cher, then go along the D956. In both these cases it would be easiest, once at Valençay, to take the D15 towards Vicq-sur-Nahon and then turn down the D15A to neighbouring Veuil just before Vicq. However, you might be coming from the direction of Loches in Touraine, in which case the Touraine D760 becomes the D960 in the Indre *département*. Some 4km after Luçay-le-Mâle along this road, change on to the little D128 to Veuil.

L'Auberge St-Fiacre

L'Auberge St-Fiacre, 36600 Veuil, Valençay, © 02 54 40 32 78. Closed Tues eve and all day Wed, except if public hols. Lunchtime menu at 98F, Mon–Sat, except on public holidays. Other menus at 130F, 185F and 225F.

Veuil, an extraordinarily well-flowered village, is so diminutive that you can't miss the Auberge St-Fiacre. It sits very prettily by the stream that passes through the village's little valley, providing water for a fountain. The church lies close by. It's dedicated to St-Pierre, not to St-Fiacre, the latter being the patron saint of gardeners, to whom the whole village seems to be devoted. The brown gravel courtyard outside the inn is shaded by a lovely horse chestnut tree. White painted iron chairs and tables are laid out outside. The little cart with a barrel forces the rustic look almost to the point of a chocolate box scene.

Inside, the inn feels dark and atmospheric. The green paint has been given a deliberate faded look. Ruddy square tiles cover the floor. There were even tiles on the window sill by which we ate. It was graced with a gilded clock and romantic scenes depicted on porcelain. Old beams above our heads, a fireplace close to hand, it was all very cosy. Many of the objects used to decorate the restaurant have been chosen by the chef's brother-in-law, who is an antiques dealer.

The chef, Jean-Louis Broquet, is Parisian by birth, and his wife from Orléans. She caused him to come down this way. With this restaurant, which they've held since the mid 1980s, he's now dragged her into the profession. She selects the wines as well as looking after the service. They fell in love with the *auberge* as soon as they saw it. They have three daughters—they say they haven't found the recipe for making boys!—and live at the inn, which dates back to the 17th century. Apparently the Spanish princes in exile stopped here one day and suffered from the consequences of eating too much melon. There is still an annual *foire aux melons de St-Fiacre* one day in August.

We decided to try one of the little-known Valençay red wines with our meal. Light in colour, fruity on the nose, it had aromas reminiscent of glacé cherries. The wine appellations of the Berry generally were well represented on the *carte des vins*, especially good but unsung *appellations* like Menetou-Salon and Reuilly. There was a decent selection of half bottles too, a good thing if you're eating *à deux*.

There's a lovely French expression to describe when people go out of their way to prepare a sumptuous meal: *mettre les petits plats dans les grands*, 'to put the little plates in the large ones'. This is definitely what goes on with the Auberge St-Fiacre. There were four plates one on top of the other in front of each of us as we tried our goat's cheese *amuse gueule* with the apéritif.

All the menus are extremely good value, but as this inn is a little off the beaten track, the chef doesn't propose a great array of choices. In fact there are no choices. You'll have to hope you like everything on one or other of the menus. The cheaper menu started with *médaillons* of smoked salmon in a salad set off not by lemon or lime juice, but by orange zest, for a change. The starter on the 180F menu was langoustines wrapped up in thin fried batter, crisply satisfying, with a salad covered in sesame seeds. With the more elaborate menu, you get a fish dish before the meat. Ours was a fish mousse sausage made from Breton pollock, very light and white, served with a delicate fish sauce and a rice cake made up of yellow and brown rice. Some of the fish that you may find on the menu may come from the lakes of the Parc Naturel Régional de la Brenne not far to the southeast in the Indre *département*, such as the *silure*.

Jean-Louis Broquet likes to describe his cuisine as half classical, half modern. He might for example serve a fish with a carrot and ginger sauce, *sandre* with pear and cinnamon, or flavour kid's liver with cumin. With an ostrich-rearing farm in the south of the *département*, you may even find that unusual bird on the menu. But he likes to prepare traditional sauces too, such as the *sauce Choron*, a béarnaise sauce with tomato purée added, or *sauce ivrogne* (drunkard's sauce), a reduction of shallots and red wine. As to Berry honey, it can occasionally pop up in any course, entrée, *plat de résistance*, or pudding!

Light piped music accompanied our conversation. It seemed the kind of intimate restaurant, with only six tables in the dining room in which we sat, where people speak in slightly subdued tones. But the atmosphere is relaxed, and through one door you can see into one of the family rooms.

The meat course on the 180F menu was a beef steak covered in a Bercy, not a Berry sauce. Otherwise it was a piece of leg of lamb served with a mustard sauce. Both were accompanied by a selection of vegetables. The cheeses were local and served to perfection. There was of course goat's cheese from Valençay, or from Anjouin to be more precise, a village east of Valençay along the D13 (you can visit the goat farm of La Prunelaye there) and a pleasing Olivet covered in peppers.

A typical problem with not being offered a choice may come with dessert. The 180F menu proposed *nougat glacé au coulis de framboises* (raspberries). Very nice and sweet, but some of us would have preferred the *gâteau moelleux aux figues et amandes*. You might feel you want to negotiate, or simply to choose *à la carte*, but then the price goes up considerably.

Magret de Canard au Miel du Berry

Serves 4

4 duck breasts
50g/2oz chopped shallots
4 tablespoons sherry vinegar
250ml/8fl oz duck or game stock
50g/2oz Berry acacia honey or other runny honey

Trim the duck breasts. Make light criss-crossing cuts into the fat with a knife. Cook them in, preferably, a cast-iron frying pan or casserole or otherwise in a heavy-bottomed frying pan over a medium heat. Cook them first on the fatty side for 10 minutes, moving them from time to time. Turn them over and cook them on the other side for 5 minutes. Then remove them from the pan with a slotted spoon and leave them to rest on a warmed plate for 10 minutes before cutting them into slices. Keep warm.

Sweat the shallots in the same pan or casserole you used to cook the duck, in the juices rendered by the duck. Deglaze the pan or casserole with the sherry vinegar, then add the honey and stock. Leave to reduce by half, then serve, dribbled over the slices of duck.

---

touring around

First, to the **Château de Valençay** (*open 9–12 and 2–6, or nightfall for the grounds*). In history, it is most famously linked with Napoleonic times and Napoleon's massively powerful foreign minister Talleyrand. But the outer façades of the building were constructed in the main during the 16th-century French Renaissance. Valençay is generally considered a typical château of the Loire Valley, mixing late Gothic and French Renaissance forms.

The two main features which immediately stand out are the château's keep and the great solid pepper-pot towers on one side, the latter the hallmark of Valençay. The keep, really a redundant military element left over from medieval architectural design, has been revised here and embellished with Renaissance features, including the Italianate classical order of columns. The extraordinarily shaped great west corner tower, though its rounded bulk again recalls shows of medieval might, is also from the 16th century.

Walk into the grand inner courtyard and the scene changes somewhat. The main wing here and the other great tower were built at the start of the 18th century. The refined windows are divided into bays by strong pilasters which span two storeys. On the typical Mansard-style split roof, arched-pediment *lucarnes* alternate with the *œil de bœuf* window. Stone urns stick out for added adornment. To the south views open on to the little Nahon valley, while east lie the château's vineyard and the town.

Although Napoleon is once supposed to have said of Talleyrand that *'C'est de la merde dans un bas de soie'* (He's shit in a silk stocking.), the man was one of the emperor's greatest ministers as well as surely one of the greatest opportunists in French history. Napoleon also said of Talleyrand that *'Il a été le plus capable de tous mes Ministres.'* When serving the emperor as his foreign minister, he was in effect given the Château de Valençay by Napoleon: 'I want you to buy a beautiful property...and that an invitation there should be a reward for the ambassadors of those sovereigns with whom I am pleased.' Valençay was the property chosen.

The guided visit around the grand interiors of the Château de Valençay concentrates a good deal on Talleryrand. You're given spicy details of his private life as well as his public one by the extremely witty guides. Talleyrand married Catherine Worlée, born in India. Her beauty is shown in a famous portrait of her at the château, painted by the female artist Vigée Le Brun. But Catherine apparently had a stupidity to match her looks. One unfortunately ambiguous phrase attributed to her came in her response to a question about her origins: *'Je suis d'Inde,'* ('I am from India/a turkey,') she explained, laying herself open to ridicule. She was said to have *'pas plus d'esprit qu'une rose'* ('no more intellect than a rose'). Although Princesse de Talleyrand, she was easily supplanted in her husband's affections by the wife of Talleyrand's nephew, his 'dear niece', as one euphemistic phrase had it, a driven, intelligent woman who came to reign with Talleyrand at Valençay. They entertained royally and liberally, the famous cook Carême among those in their service.

You can wander around Valençay's grounds. The park is populated by a whole menagerie of animals, while a large makeshift outbuilding also holds an extensive and impressive collection of old cars. The other main attraction in Valençay itself is a posh hotel and restaurant, the reputed Hôtel d'Espagne, 9 rue du Château (✆ 02 54 00 00 02), based around a former coaching inn.

After lunch you might go for a quick wander around the village of Veuil. If you climb the hill to circle the ruined château, from the height you can spot the Château de Valençay. You may also come across the monument to Resistance members shot dead here in 1944.

The village church has a typical Berry Romanesque defensive helmeted steeple. There's a stained glass window representing St Fiacre inside. He is said to have been a 7th-century royal Celt who travelled to France with his sister to take up a pious life. He supposedly turned down a crown when his father died and fed the poor and the sick who came to be healed by him in his hermitage where he grew vegetables for his visitors!

In the afternoon head southeastwards from Veuil for the **Château de Bouges** (*open July and Aug, 10–1 and 2–7; June 10–12 and 2–7, closed Tues; April, May, June and Sept, 10–12 and 2–6, closed Tues; Mar and Nov, weekends only, 10–12 and 2–5*), crossing the D956 to get on to the D37 to reach it. This château is pure elegance, in fact like a rather suave architectural box set down in the Indre countryside. A simple classical rectangle, it is often described as resembling Versailles's Petit Trianon. It is thought possible that Jacques Ange Gabriel, one of the Versailles architects, or his pupil Fayette may have had a hand in the designs. The château was built in 1762 for the Count Charles Le Blanc de Marnaval, an owner of ironworks. His family didn't benefit from it long, and from 1818 to 1826 it too fell into Talleyrand's grasping hands.

Within the box are kept the elegant accoutrements of mainly 18th-century and some 19th-century noble living. The place is beautifully furnished, with many pieces revealing something of past aristocratic ways and family life: a man's dressing table for powdering his wig; a *voyeuse* chair for women in vast crinolines to watch the society games comfortably; the library ladder which folds away impeccably into the leather-covered stool; and a 19th-century *fermage* or rent farmer's table, with a turning drawer to avoid the vulgarity of passing money from hand to hand. The *semainier*, with a drawer for each day of the week, was apparently replaced by a *décadier* (one of which you can see here) during the Revolution, as the unit of the week was changed to ten-day periods—will the European Union ever take that one up and try to introduce some weird, ingenious metrical system for European days?

In season, cut flowers from the garden adorn many rooms while the generous grounds invite you to an afternoon stroll.

Goats in Clover in the Cher Valley

Ferme - Auberge Bouland

The Loire Valley is almost as much about the great tributaries of the Loire as the majestic river itself. The Cher is one of the most important currents to add its weight to the Loire's waters, joining it near Tours. The Cher boasts the most beautiful bridge in the world, of course, the Château de Chenonceau.

Chenonceau lies on the eastern border of Touraine. This is a day spent along the Cher valley just east of it. Here the river is much quieter, with few of the tourist pilgrimage buses continuing this far. The next Cher royal stop east of Chenonceau is Montrichard, with one of those imposing early medieval keeps that mark the Loire Valley landscape from time to time. Here it has to hold its own against the town's modern architecture. The birds of prey frequently seen circling round the tower aren't wild, but part of the tourist falconry attractions.

Several charming little sites lie lost in the countryside around Montrichard: the Château de Montpoupon, dedicated to the hunt; the Abbaye of Pontlevoy, an abbey that appears simply to have gone awol in the vineyards of the Cher valley; and the Château du Gué-Péan, a fairy-tale of a château if ever there was one, with one unforgettable bell-shaped tower to fall in love with once you've cut your way through the thick woods that surround it. The road down the hillside from Gué-Péan leads back down into the Cher valley and to the Gallo-Roman settlement at Thésée, only small fragments of which are left. Carrying on along the Cher's north bank to St-Aignan, you come to a beautiful riverside and hillside town.

Just south of St-Aignan lies the Zooparc de Beauval, a serious zoo best-known for its white tigers, aviary and seal shows. The Cher valley roads continues east to Selles, with its two châteaux in one, but that small town is most famed for its goat's cheese, a great Loire speciality, and one of the main reasons for choosing the *ferme auberge* that we have for lunch.

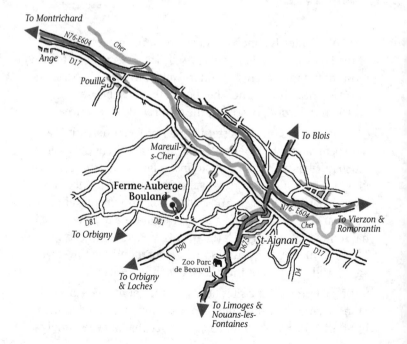

Mareuil lies between St-Aignan and Montrichard, on the south bank of the Cher. St-Aignan is the closer of the two towns, only 4½ km from the village. The Ferme Auberge Bouland is actually some way south of Mareuil, roughly the same distance again, lost in the countryside. In Mareuil, turn down by the *boulangerie* and follow the signposts; you have to go roughly 4km, some of the route taking you between Cher vineyards, before you see signs for a left turn. A little way along this new road and another left turn takes you down to the *ferme auberge*.

Ferme Auberge Bouland

Ferme Auberge Bouland, La Lionnière, 41110 Mareuil-sur-Cher,
℮ 02 54 75 24 99, ℮ 02 54 75 44 74. Open every day except Mon.
(Only open Mon when a public hol.) You must reserve a table at least a day
in advance out of season. Menus go from 88F to 140F. The price depends
on the meat served. Normally it's 88F for a weekday meal, 98F at weekends
and on public holidays or if leg or shoulder of goat or lamb is served; the
price goes up to 110F for kid, 125F for freshwater fish. For a meal at 140F
offering both a meat and a fish course you need to order specially.

Goat's cheese, as you'll quickly realize, is a culinary passion across the Loire Valley and there's no better place to try the stuff in its varied forms, from soft, gentle, creamy white to explosive toffee-brown, than at the Ferme Auberge Bouland. Almost all the food the *ferme auberge* serves is produced either on the farm or in the neighbourhood.

The atmosphere at a *ferme auberge* should be rural and relaxed, and that is what it's like at Frédéric and Françoise Bouland's. Madame is from the Loir-et-Cher while Monsieur is of Parisian origins. They took over this farm in the mid 1970s. It had been abandoned, so they had to do it up, trying to keep its old character. They started up the *ferme auberge* early in the 1980s. Madame looks after much of the cooking while Monsieur is quietly in charge of the service.

You eat in a converted farm building, with a long, narrow, basic conservatory giving onto the garden, or in the garden itself. This is a charming, slightly unkempt corner, full of hydrangea, hollyhocks, lilies, marguerites, a rose arch... and with the odd fruit tree providing shade for tables and benches. The French have an expression for this kind of little semi-trained paradise: a *jardin de curé*, a village priest's garden.

The farm courtyard by which you enter is kept clean and tidy. A mix of plants in pots is scattered on the red tiles by the main doorway. On the wall above, an old sculpture of a horse's head indicates that this part of the farm used to be the stables. The main objects of the owners' affections today are the goats. The goat sheds lie at the bottom of the sloping yard. You could go and take a look at them before lunch if they're around. There are some 120 *chèvres* on the farm, plus around 30 ewes (*brebis* in French). You can distinguish two types of goats. The brown ones are *alpines*. They also have blackened faces and a black stripe along the back. The white variety are Saanen goats. Some are a mix—the Boulands say that they're encouraging a multiracial society! You should also be able to see fowl clucking about the farm. All the farm animals are reared in the old-fashioned way.

It certainly does help to like goat in all its forms if you come to eat here. The creatures not only make up the main herd on the farm but also the main feature on the menus. These menus are extremely simple and cheap, but very filling and satisfying. As well as goat meat, you may be offered the choice of lamb, duck, chicken or guinea fowl. Freshwater fish is also a possibility...and let's not forget kid (*chevreau*), by way of a change. But what is on the menu depends on the farm's supplies, so you have to be accommodating.

The service can be quite slow, so don't get impatient. The owners stress that part of the experience is that you should relax on the farm and accept an older, more rural pace of life and eating, rather than frantically trying to rush down your food before another manic dash to another château. *Détente,* by the way, which features on the menu, is the French for relaxation.

On to the food itself. There are six elements to the menu. You are first offered a *kir maison,* a cocktail of local Mareuil Sauvignon produced from organic grapes combined with *crème de cassis.* This *crème de cassis*, blackcurrant liqueur, is made from fruit from the farm and its neighbours. For the starter, you may be served a mixture of *crudités*, the typical French entrée of various vegetables served with vinaigrette. More likely it'll be a salad with cold goat's cheese, maybe fresh, maybe grated from a piece that has gone through the process of cheese ripening, *affinage*.

Mme. Bouland explains how some of their dry goat's cheese is made. The cheese is placed in layers in an earthenware pot known as a *tinette*. The layers of cheese are separated by chestnut leaves—vine leaves aren't used as they'll have been treated in some way. The pot is covered with a cork. The cheese is then left in a darkened corner to develop, turning *moelleux* and becoming increasingly full-bodied and piquant. When it's well done, Mme. Bouland compares the cheese to a parmesan. This is the kind of cheese she may grate over the salads.

The next course is a bit of a bonus, essentially a second starter, when you can try the delicious *beignets au chèvre*, for example, the recipe for which is given below. Or you may be offered a homemade pâté, perhaps made with pork, or more exotically, possibly with deer liver. Then again you may be treated to a slice of *tarte au chèvre*. In this, blue goat's cheese is mixed with fromage frais, crème fraîche, flour, eggs, seasoning and lots of chives, with a little more of that well done cheese already mentioned to pep up the taste.

The main course depends on what is ready, as has already been explained. The *coq au Sauvignon* is one of the best dishes. It makes a change from all those chickens in red wine; looking and tasting lighter than the thick-sauced old favourite. Ineluctably we move to the cheese course (as though we hadn't had a couple of cheese courses already!). Among the selection you'll find some of the most amazingly strong, dark brown toffee-like stuff, the most powerful goat's cheese you're ever likely to taste—try the minutest portions only, remembering the incident in *Asterix in Corsica* where a cheese blows up a boat.

It may come as a slight relief to you to hear that we didn't spot any goat's cheese in the puddings. You may be served a nice egg custard however. Or a *clafoutis*, a flan, freshened with fruits from the farm.

The *prunes acides* are the tasty plums which appear the earliest in the garden. Other days you might be offered apple fritters, or a sponge cake with strawberries or raspberries, again grown very locally.

Beignets au Fromage de Chèvre

Serves 4

2 eggs
300g/11oz self-raising flour
4 small individual Loire or other French goat's cheeses
250ml/8fl oz milk
salt and pepper
small handful fresh chives, finely chopped
oil, for deep-frying
1 small lettuce or selection of salad leaves, washed and trimmed

Mix the eggs with the flour. Add the milk little by little, mixing the batter until it is smooth. Season to taste with salt and pepper and add the chives. Roll the goat's cheeses in the batter until they are well coated. Heat sufficient oil in which to deep-fry the cheeses, then gently put them into very hot oil. Turn them over frequently until they have browned on all sides. Serve hot on a bed of the salad leaves.

touring around

Like a decadent parody of a Jacob's ladder, a magnificent monumental staircase lined with trees climbs from St-Aignan's church porch not up to heaven but to the **château of St-Aignan.** The town is very appealing, the nicest spot on the Cher after Chenonceau and Villandry, and from the splendid château terrace you get a fine view of it. On one side it tumbles down the slope to the river, the valley stretching north into the distance. On the other side, the old town roofs, a mix of brown tiles and slate, pop up out of the cramped tributary valley. It's not possible to visit the interior of the château, but while up on its grandiose platform you can admire its excellent French Renaissance *lucarnes.*

An island lies in the middle of the Cher, *l'île aux trois évêques*, or the island of the three bishops, indicating the ancient divide between the territories of the dioceses of Orléans, Tours and Bourges. Aignan, after whom the town is named, was the bishop of Orléans who saved that city from Attila the Hun. Now the island is the location for a tourist office and a Maison du Vin. You can also take a boat trip down the Cher from the beach area, or hire canoes or pedalos.

Descending the château staircase, you're led straight into the great narthex of the **church of St-Aignan** below. Inside, 19th-century restorers have had their cleansing way, operating on the space to give it an almost hospital-like whiteness. For a recorded commentary on the church, on the left as you enter there's a button which activates a 15-minute recorded guided tour. The capitals in the choir look absurdly sparkling and new. Though their decoration follows the traditional forms of entertaining Romanesque representation, they're 19th-century re-creations. The high point of the church interior is the crypt. This was in fact an older church, upon which the larger one above was plonked. Its dark, dank space contains some fine vestiges of Romanesque wall paintings and capitals and offered excellent conditions for a local wine merchant to keep his stock in the last century, saving this level from the clinical restoration work above.

The most original painting, in the southern ambulatory chapel, depicts events not in the life of St Aignan but in that of St Gilles. Here he performs acts of charity and miracles, clothing a beggar, healing a man bitten by a snake and even praying powerfully enough to rescue a ship from being wrecked. The St Gilles artist is thought to have painted the grandiose Christ in Majesty in the inner apse chapel. This is a movingly composed piece, showing Christ enthroned, flanked to the sides of the mandorla by St Peter and St James Minor, who appear to bow before his glory thanks to the curve of the apse. At the feet of their robes cripples grovel, one with a stick holding out a coin, another moving along on walking irons. The frescoes to the side of this powerful scene are much later, from the 15th century, but also show penitent, frail mortals, the lord of St-Aignan, Louis II de Chalon, and his second wife Jeanne de Perellos. They caused a terrible scandal in 1420 when they eloped from the Burgundian court—Louis was unfortunately already married to Marie de la Trémouille. Further up from the Romanesque painting on this vault is a 16th-century inter-pretation of the Last Judgement, what Louis and Jeanne might well have lived in fear of.

Clearly marked south from St-Aignan, the well-run **Zooparc de Beauval** (*open 9–nightfall*) all started with an innocent-sounding request which should act as a cautionary tale to all parents visiting with their children. Madame Delors was asked by her three-year-old daughter whether they could keep a couple of birds in their Paris apartment. Now she runs this seriously large, serious-minded and well-flowered zoo with her children. One of the strengths of the park is a sizeable new aviary full of tropical birds. The parrots tend to come from Parisian owners who got sick of their pets, as do some of the more dangerous animals—Beauval also serves as something of an animal sanctuary. The parrot was prized as a possession rarer than many a fabulous jewel by the Loire kings of France. Along with the booty and artists Charles VIII brought back with him from his Italian foray at the end of the 15th century was a Moor from Naples, recruited as *garde des perroquets du roi*. In the mammals section of the zoo, the wild cats are particularly impressive.

If you'd like to visit one of the vineyards supplying wine to the *ferme auberge* at very good value, one of the best addresses to visit around lunchtime would be the Clos Roche Blanche near Mareuil. The wine cellar is dug into the rock, while the vines, tended biologically, grow on slopes dominating the Cher valley.

Head on in the afternoon to the **Château du Gué-Péan**. This château (*open April–Sept, 9am–7pm; rest of year, 10–6*) is not quite cut off by impenetrable woods and brambles, but at least lost down dark tracks, the meadows around it surrounded by the forest of Choussy. To reach it, head up the slope of the Cher valley west of Thésée past Monthou-sur-Cher—look out carefully for the tiny signs marking the way.

Gué-Péan means 'paying ford', but it's hard to imagine anyone forking out money to come by such obscure backroads in centuries past. A joy to look at from the outside, the château seems somewhat dejected in parts, even badly run down at the back, but it's full of charm. Each corner is marked by a solid tower, one distinguishing itself remarkably from the rest. Comparisons with a bell, a pepper-pot or even a German military helmet don't seem wholly absurd given its faintly ridiculous appearance. It's both distinctive and comical, medieval and Renaissance. As well as the towers, the front section of buildings in the courtyard (up until the end of the pavilions) dates from the middle of the 16th century. Inside, the rooms have been sadly impoverished by a burglary in the mid-1990s, but you're shown a string of elegant *salons* in the main wing.

Continuing the culinary and troglodyte theme, at **Bourré** you might visit the Caves Champignonnières (*open Easter to All Saints', guided tours at 10 and 11, and on the hour, 2–5*), where mushrooms are produced in former stone quarries. The stone of Bourré was particularly prized for its whiteness in times past. In fact it's said to grow whiter with age—you might think that's only an effect observed by those who've tried magic mushrooms. Approach Bourré from the south to appreciate the troglodyte qualities of the village. At La Magnanerie (*open April–Nov, every day except Tues, visits at 11, 2, 4 and 5*) you can learn about other uses to which the caves were converted, both for human habitation and for silkworm production.

The keep is the main attraction in **Montrichard**, and it has lured a lot more tourists since being renamed the **Donjon des Aigles** (*Eagles' keep; open 15 June–15 Sept, 10–12 and 2.30–6.30; rest of time between Easter and end Sept, afternoons only; displays of falconry, 15 June–15 Sept, every afternoon at 3.30 and 5; double-check on times before you go; you have to pay an extra fee for the show*). When not performing for the tourists, the birds are the keep's modern-day prisoners, displayed chained among the many picturesque ruined towers and walls at the base of the keep. A local museum is crammed into one tower.

If you wish to at least set eyes on the **Château de Chenonceau**, most glamorous of all the Loire châteaux, consider taking a Cher boat from Chisseaux just east of it that takes you tantalisingly close to the château?

A Halt in George Sand's Loches Stables

Loches are little fish which populate the Indre river flowing through the historic castled town of the same name. And the terrace of the Hôtel George Sand on which you can eat actually extends over the water where the small creatures swim. George Sand, the well-meaning novelist and 19th-century leading female light, apparently stabled her horses in part of this building, once a posting inn and with origins going back to the 15th century.

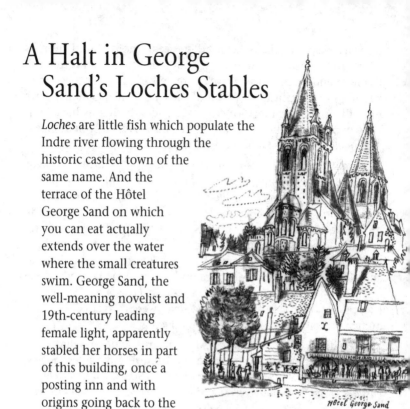

Hôtel George Sand

You could easily spend a whole morning up in the citadel of Loches. It contains not one, but two châteaux: an early medieval donjon, ravens circling round its mighty defences, and a much more liveable-in restored 15th-century royal castle. Charles VII was the Valois who adopted the town as one of his headquarters after he was forced to abandon Paris to avoid the English invasion at the start of the second half of the Hundred Years War—thus the French royal family's century based in the Loire Valley began.

The countryside and the villages around Loches are particularly enticing. The best road to take for an afternoon of touring is the D760 eastwards. This leads you through the forest of

Loches and past the memorable remnants of several former religious institutions before you arrive at Montrésor. This village is justifiably part of the association of *Les plus beaux villages de France*. Continue to the church of Nouans-les-Fontaines not for its architecture, but for one single but huge and hugely significant painting, a panel piece attributed to the first recognized great French painter, Jean Fouquet.

getting there

The Hôtel George Sand sits right by the Indre below Loches's royal citadel. Loches lies along the N143 between Tours and Châteauroux, 41km from the Touraine capital. If you're coming along the A10 motorway, take the Ste-Maure-de-Touraine exit and follow the D760 some 30 km east to Loches.

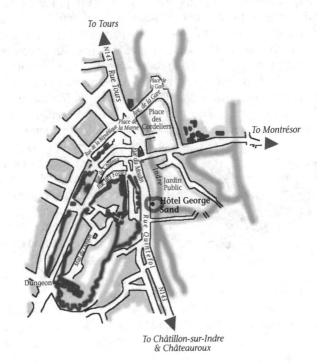

Hôtel George Sand

Hôtel George Sand, 39 rue Quintefol, 37600 Loches, ✆ 02 47 59 39 74, 🖷 02 47 91 55 75. Menus at 95F (except Sundays and public holidays), 145F, 180F, 230F and 290F.

The front of the hotel is rather too close to the road for comfort or to give it charm, but within, the dining room walls are in lovely whiter-than-white tufa limestone blocks. Bernard Fortin was previously in the construction industry, so he has been able to direct the restoration of this building, which he and his wife bought in the late 1970s, with some aplomb. The place had previously served as a restaurant, but had been abandoned some 20 years.

As explained, the link with George Sand is rather tenuous. She is a much more interesting social figure than a novelist, unfortunately more remembered for her love affair with Chopin and relationships with other eminent early 18th-century men than for her own interesting life. Loches didn't play a large part in it; her main country base was in the Berry. She would not have recognized the nicely done interior here, nor the splendid terrace over the Indre river itself—it was M. Fortin who added the latter. The two dining rooms have some nice old beams and fireplaces and the odd tapestry. Some of the little baskets in pine were made by the chef. Bernard Gauthier cares deeply about his profession; he has been a cook for over 30 years. He has worked in some very upmarket addresses, including at Chissay, nearby on the Cher, before coming here a few years ago. He says that he has stuck with traditional cooking. In particular, he has adapted a stock of old recipes from the start of the century. The recipe given here is a regional speciality, using the typical Touraine *géline*, a black hen with an impressive crest.

The menus go from the simple three-course *menu lochois* at an excellent value 85F to the elaborate *menu Frédéric Chopin* (195F) or the outrageous *menu George Sand* (245F). There's also a *menu des bords de l'Indre* at 125F. The *menu lochois* might start with a vegetable soup or seafood salad with salmon and shrimps, or you could go for a more homely scrambled eggs with French bacon. The main course is a choice between the dish of the day or, say, a slice of coley fish with oyster cream. For pudding, either goat's cheese on a bed of salad or a choice from the excellent pudding trolley.

The *menu des bords de l'Indre* is as tempting and gentle as you could imagine. The hors d'œuvre options on the day we visited had diminutive names which suggested elegant portions—even the words chosen were friendly. We could decide between *cassolette de haddock et beurre au safran,* a kind of haddock stew, or the *compotée de lapereau et sa confiture d'oignon,* the meat of sweet little rabbits mixed with equally sweet little onions. Or there was a velouté with cauliflower and smoked salmon. An imaginative start. The main course was easier to decide on, with simple accompaniments, for example a tomato coulis with the hake steak, or fresh thyme with the lamb on a skewer. Cheese or salad were then followed by pudding. As well as the selection from the dessert trolley, you could choose from a poached pear in sweet wine and chocolate sauce or hot *clafoutis,* a flan, with honey and strawberries.

But we would recommend most strongly sitting down to the *menu Frédéric Chopin,* a more sophisticated romance of cuisine. You could start with an apéritif to accompany the *assiette d'accueil,* an appetizer. By way of an entrée, perhaps a *salade folle,* a mad salad of quail, *al dente* vegetables and truffle-perfumed vinaigrette? Some of the dishes did seem to get a little carried away—the langoustines were served with a grapefruit butter and *son flan à la badiane,* a star anis-flavoured egg accompaniment, a tangy and startling combination of flavours. By comparison, the homemade duck foie gras with artichokes seemed rather simple.

The Loire fish favourite, *sandre,* was served up not only with local Gamay wine, but also with Meaux mustard to add bite. *Brochet,* pike, is another popular freshwater fish that features quite regularly on Loire Valley menus. Its firm flesh was cooked with a fine vinegar. Bass was the third fish choice, served with salsify and in a fennel sauce, the last a Provençal touch. However, the proposed two meat dishes were traditionally *tourangeau*. The *magret de canard* was cooked in a sauce with prunes. Plums used to be grown in large number in Touraine and dried to make prunes, so it's good to see dishes reminding you of this. The rich sweet taste of good prunes, and also their soft texture, contrasts especially well with the firm duck.

The other main course was a *suprême* of *géline de Touraine*. A leaflet we were given about the special Dame Noire *géline* claims that these corn-fed hens originated in Loches and that 750,000 of them were trotting around the farmyards of Touraine at one time. After a steep drop in numbers, they are now being championed again for restaurant plates.

The next town directly west of Loches, Ste-Maure-de-Touraine, is highly reputed for its goat's cheese. It has even gained the right to declare its output *appellation d'origine contrôlée*, a rare distinction given to guarantee quality and local production. Ste-Maure goat's cheese generally comes as a roll held in the centre by a straw. It's a firm, rich, slowly-melting and quite mild-tasting goat's cheese. The chef served it to us in flaky pastry and flavoured with paprika. If selecting from the cheeseboard, you might like to look out for the ewe's milk cheese from Perusson near Loches.

So to the *desserts*. Some nice Touraine touches here. What about a *tarte fine aux poires, sauce chocolat, glacé aux noix* (pear tart with choco-late sauce and walnut ice-cream)? Or there was the choice of a soup of fruits in Touraine wine with a pistachio biscuit. There are other tradi-tional French puddings too, such as chocolate gâteau, here served with an orange cream, or crème brûlée flavoured with *réglisse*, licorice. The *menu George Sand*, by contrast, adds an extra dimension (one extra course) to the full Chopin menu, with a glass of sweet white wine to accompany the foie gras, although other-wise it is very close to it.

Géline de Touraine Pochée dans son Bouillon et Rôtie au Vieux Vinaigre de Vin, Fricassée de Champignons des Bois

Serves 4–6

1 Touraine hen or boiling chicken, about 1.8–3.2kg/4–7lbs
2 litres/3 ½ pints chicken stock
100g/4oz chanterelle mushrooms
100g/4oz cep mushrooms
100g/4oz horn of plenty mushrooms
100g/4oz butter
2 garlic cloves, chopped
100g/4oz large spring onions, finely sliced
1 tablespoon chopped fresh parsley
100ml/4fl oz aged wine vinegar
1 shallot, chopped
150g/5oz crème fraîche

Poach the chicken gently, covered in the chicken stock, for 2 hours. Reserve 150ml/¼ pint of the remainiong liquid. Preheat the oven to 200°C/400°F (gas mark mark 6). Take the chicken out of the broth, cut it into quarters and roast them in the preheated oven for 15–20 minutes. Meanwhile, sauté the mushrooms in a frying pan in half the butter, together with the garlic, spring onions and parsley. Season to taste and keep warm.

Put the vinegar into a saucepan with the shallot and cook until the liquid has reduced by half. Add the reserved cooking liquor and let it reduce by half. Mix in the cream, bring to the boil and whisk in the remaining butter.

Place the chicken in a serving dish, spoon the mushrooms around it and put the sauce in a gravy boat. Serve piping hot.

touring around

The counts of Anjou won the stronghold site of Loches' **Château** and **Donjon** (*opening hours vary slightly for the two, except July–mid-Sept. Times stated here are for the château; outside of July–mid-Sept, add an extra half-hour for the keep closing times. July–mid-Sept, 9–7; mid-*

March–June and mid–end Sept, 9–12 and 2–6; Oct–Dec and Feb–mid-March, 9–12 and 2–5; closed Jan) through marriage, not war, in the 10th century. Given Loches's easterly position it became an important outpost for them in their territorial conflict with the counts of Blois. It was an obvious hill for fortifications and the first remaining ones probably date from the great Foulques Nerra of Anjou, built possibly as early as the 1030s. Royal connections came from the time of Henri Plantagenêt. Henri, Angevin king of England as Henry II, added greatly to the earlier defences, in particular with the building of ramparts and the digging of a great ditch, still to be seen. French king Philippe Auguste's men won Loches back from King John and the English Crown in 1205 after a terrible one-year siege—the citadel did at least have its own well to help its defenders. The end of the siege brought to a close Plantagenet control in this region. Through the 13th century, the Loches fortifications were reinforced with *tours à bec*, beak-pointed towers, and further military architecture was added in the course of the 14th and 15th centuries. The royal lodgings, at the other end of the outcrop, date from the 14th and 15th centuries. Expansion continued around the keep, however. The great Tour Neuve is something of a second donjon in its own right. Nearby, the Martelet, from Charles VII's reign, burrows underground into former quarries to provide three levels of cells. These towers have a very dark reputation in history, associated with King Louis XI's cruelty. A further surround of 16th-century positions completed the hilltop defences.

It makes sense in historical terms to start the tour with the keep, reached by an arrowhead-shaped barbican and a drawbridge. With outer walls puckered with beam holes for the scaffolding needed for its construction and with black jackdaws circling round the sheer walls, the place looks forbidding and impregnable. Awe-inspiring, it's considered the finest example of a keep from the Romanesque period in France. It was of course lived in in medieval times.

Loches's keep and towers have been converted into something of a museum on torture and imprisonment. Louis IX—otherwise ironically known as Saint Louis, as he was sanctified by the Catholic Church for his crusading work—formalized the use of torture. After the death of Charles VII, who had held court at Loches, his son Louis XI, who clearly had bad memories of the place, converted it in good part into a prison, which it remained for centuries. Terrible tales survive of men holed up in Loches's *oubliettes* (from the French *oublier*, to forget). The most famous prisoner here was Ludovico Sforza, at the start of the 16th century. An extremely powerful and ruthless Italian lord, one-time patron of Leonardo da Vinci, he got on the wrong side of the French when the Valois tried to lay claim to certain desirable parts of Italy. Sforza ended his days in Loches, although not in the awful conditions claimed by legend. To go by the art daubed on the walls of his cell he was certainly allowed paints, among other luxuries.

For the other, easier side of life at the Château de Loches, you need to go to the other end of the promontory, to the *logis royal*. The delightful statues of dogs greeting you at the entrance are 19th-century stone pets. The lodgings are made up of two adjoining wings of different style, the first built at the end of the 14th century, the other at the end of the 15th to the beginning of the 16th. The main Charles VII section was the celebrated home for Charles VII's powerful mistress, Agnès Sorel, she of the single bared breast immortalized in work by France's greatest known 15th-century painter, Jean Fouquet. Agnès Sorel was a woman who stirred the passions, both greatly loved and profoundly hated in her time. Winning the king's affections, she exercised political as well as emotional power over him. She had already been in the service of Isabelle de Lorraine, wife of René d'Anjou, when in 1444 she entered the royal court retinue as a lady-in-waiting to the queen. Soon it was the queen, Marie d'Anjou, who would have to wait to see the king. Breaking with traditional etiquette, the king had Agnès Sorel served like a princess, allowing her a retinue of her own. Agnès Sorel bore the king three daughters herself.

Agnès Sorel wasn't the only influential woman to leave her mark on Loches. Two other of the most memorable women in French history are associated with the castle. Joan of Arc came to Loches after the French victory freeing Orléans from the English siege. Here she spurred on Charles VII to go through English-occupied territory to be crowned in the sacred French royal ceremony at Rheims cathedral. His sacred crowning helped to assert his perceived divine right to rule France. Anne de Bretagne is the third great woman whose spirit remains over Loches. Pious wife of two French kings, Charles VIII and Louis XII, her oratory is the best preserved of the rooms in a rather bare series, several containing some uninspiring copies of famous paintings. Before leaving the citadel, take a look at the church of St-Ours with the curious *dubes*, those central cones rising above the nave.

Taking the D760 east from Loches you enter what was once the ancient royal **forest of Loches**. At the crossroads with the D9 you come across the surprise of an obelisk in the woods. This is one in a line of them along a diagonal forest path, set up as elegant markers for the hunt in the 18th century. You then pass La Corroirie, the gorgeous mellow medieval buildings opposite a waterlily-covered lake that were once the monastic dwellings for the lay brothers of the charterhouse, separated by quite some distance from the monks' quarters. The main monastery or **Chartreuse du Liget** (*private property now, but generally easy to visit by asking permission at one of the top houses*) is much grander, great lengths of walls with the occasional little turret surrounding the buildings.

Henry II is purported to have founded this institution in 1178 as part of his penance for the murder of Thomas à Becket in Canterbury Cathedral in 1170. But this entrance is pure 18th-century and the bulk of the collection of buildings that curiously descend the slope are either 17th or 18th, ending in the picturesque 17th-century central section, still lived in. At the bottom of the valley, at an angle to the other architecture, the substantial remains of a late 12th-century church still stand. To the west of that, you walk through the gateway into the vestiges of a truly vast 17th-century cloister.

Montrésor exudes charm from every stone. A very quiet village of brown-tiled houses, it is situated in a curve of a tributary of the Indre, the Indrois, overseen by a fortified castle. The **château** (*open April–Oct, 10–12 and 2–6*) merits a visit, if only for the views on to the village houses by the Indrois, their small segments of gardens a jumble down to the tree-lined meander in the river. A legend ascribes the name of the town, Mount Treasure, to the unlikely emergence from the local rock of a lizard covered in gold. You need look no further than the château for some rather extraordinary treasures from the east—eastern Europe that is. The many Polish street names are explained by the family that owns the castle. Head on to Nouans if you wish to see Jean Fouquet's moving depiction of Christ's descent from the cross that dominates the interior of the village church.

A Conspiratorial Château outside Amboise

The name of Amboise is inextricably associated with French royalty to this day, so it seems only appropriate to choose a rather noble château for lunch in the area. Not only is Noizay close to Amboise. It is also near to the splendid city of Tours and right next to the Vouvray wine district. It's not right next to the Loire, though, but sits above the Cisse, a tributary that borrows one side of its great brother's bed. A

Le Château de Noizay

charming meadow-lined road runs along the Cisse parallel to the Loire from the Touraine border until close to Tours.

Amboise was the scene of one of the first truly dreadful outbursts of violent tensions between Huguenots and Catholics in 16th-century France. The *conjuration d'Amboise*, or Amboise plot, was something of a precursor of the Wars of Religion, which tore France apart from the 1560s to the end of the century. The Château de Noizay was deeply implicated in the plot.

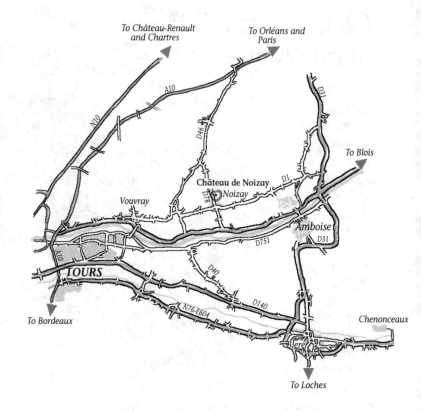

getting there

The Château de Noizay, in the village of Noizay, lies along the discreet Cisse valley between Nazelles-Négron and Vouvray. Looking at a general map of France, you'll find Vouvray between Tours and Amboise, on the north side of the Loire. Note that there's no road bridge between Tours and Amboise (the crossing at Vouvray is for trains), so make sure you get onto the Loire north bank in either of those towns to avoid a round-about journey and being unfashionably late for lunch. If you're coming from the A10 motorway, either take the exit north of Tours, or the one for Amboise, whichever's more convenient.

Château de Noizay

Château de Noizay, 37210 Noizay, ✆ 02 47 52 11 01, 📠 02 47 52 04 64. Closed 4 Jan–mid-March. Menus at 150F (lunchtime only), 240F, 270F and 360F.

Noizay is one of those delightful kinds of spots where the terrors of history have given way to the gentler temptations of tourism. The driveway to this restored 16th-century château takes you into a little park with large shady trees and leads you round to the entrance. You can see how impressive cellars have been cut into the hillside.

As you approach Noizay from the south, you may note that this quiet little village in fact contains not one, but two châteaux. The one to the east is in typical Loire white stone, with typical flashy turrets. The Château de Noizay is less showy, with an uncharacteristic fawn colour dominating the façades, but with windows surrounded by white tufa. The colours of the village church match our château.

The Château de Noizay is a member of that élite association of hotels known as Relais & Châteaux. This group boasts many of the very finest hotels in France as its members. They can sometimes be a bit intimidating and formal. The staff and waiters will normally be immaculately turned out, and you can imagine them being scolded in quiet corners for the slightest peccadillo. Actually, many of the Relais & Châteaux aren't as snobbish as you might imagine. The Château de Noizay is one of those. And beyond its intimate size and character, we found the cuisine here fantastic. Our meal included eating one of the very best desserts we tried along the Loire, reproduced below.

The place is run with appreciable courtesy by François Mollard. Five generations have followed each other in the profession. François Mollard's great-great-grandfather, from the Auvergne, went up to Paris to make his fortune and opened a *bistrot* which became the famous Brasserie Mollard. François's father moved to Touraine, buying the Château de Marçay. This is now looked after by François's brother Philippe, as is Les Hautes Roches, the most extraordinary and upmarket troglodyte hotel in the Loire, at Rochecorbon close to Noizay. François Mollard was working in the Plaza Athénée, what the French call a *palace*, a top class hotel which puts an emphasis on the finest service, when his brother asked him if he'd come to work in the Loire Valley in 1990. The chef here, Didier Frébou, is from the region and has been at Noizay since 1992. His cooking is extremely refined.

The setting is very refined too. The lovely entrance hall with its chequered flooring contains an impressive staircase. This staircase is of chestnut wood, splendidly wonky. It's worth taking a slightly disorientating few paces up it to admire the whole hall. Stained glass windows depict the leaders of the conflicting parties in the conspiracy of Amboise in which Noizay played such a large part, Huguenot La Renaudie and ultra-Catholic *Ligue* leader the duc de Guise. Tapestries, deer heads and armour all make for classic Loire château interior decoration. You could take an apéritif in one of the château's elegant salons. Although François Mollard is happy to see people in casual wear, it's best to avoid shorts and sandals in such surrounds.

Now Relais & Châteaux restaurants aren't cheap. But at lunchtime you can try the delicious cooking at Noizay for a not unreasonable 150F. And this menu includes both an *amuse bouche* to start with and coffee and *mignardises* to end, so you can't say that it's ungenerous. However, you don't get a choice of dishes with this menu. Nor do you with the *menu régional* at 240F. However, this was outstanding when we ate here. The entrée got things off to a fine start. Pigeon can be one of the most deliciously flavoursome of all meats. Here it was *mi-fumé*, semi-smoked, and served with Touraine mushrooms and *rillons*. *Rillons* are a typically *tourangeau* pork speciality. In the great Touraine writer Balzac's *Le Lys dans la vallée*, the deprived protagonist writes ruefully about being tormented by his classmates with their *rillons*, symbols of their more caring families, when he's sent off to boarding school. 'They licked their lips, saying how delicious the *rillons* were, those pieces of pork sautéd in fat and which resemble cooked truffles...'

Do I even need to tell you what the main course was? Yes, *sandre*. To bring it out, a sauce made with Chinon wine and *moutarde violette*. But at Noizay the zander was in no way dry or hard. You can guess what the cheese dish was too, goat's cheese, served hot with a salad containing walnuts, the latter also formerly a common harvest in Touraine. The pudding was supremely good, using the local Vouvray wine with its characteristic tingling quality. Try making it yourselves.

The regional menu changes with the seasons. Another time you might try asparagus wrapped in smoked salmon or mixed stuffed Loire vegetables in a marjoram sauce, Lochois ewe's milk cheese with fresh herbs, and a crackly strawberry *millefeuille aux fraises sur son miroir au vin de Chinon*. Even the puddings' names can sound romantic in these surrounds. With the *menu dégustation* and *à la carte* things just get more and more luxurious, but then you have to pay the price.

Crémets d'Anjou aux Pruneaux, Granité au Vouvray Pétillant

Serves 4

For the crémets d'Anjou:
250g/9oz fromage blanc (40% fat content)
120g/4½oz thick crème fraîche
400g/14oz sugar
3 egg whites
150g/5oz stoned prunes, cubed, plus a few to decorate
10g/¼oz powdered liquorice

For the granité au Vouvray pétillant:
750ml/1¼ pints water
750ml/1¼ pints sparkling Vouvray
250g/9oz sugar

*First make the **crémets d'Anjou**. Whisk the fromage blanc, cream and 100g/4oz of the sugar together. Then, beat the egg whites until they stiffen. As they start to harden and become dry, gradually add the remaining sugar. Gently fold the sweetened egg whites into the fromage blanc and cream mixture. Add the prunes cut into large cubes and powdered liquorice. Spoon the mixture into a square of muslin or cheese-cloth and suspend over a bowl for 4 hours.*

*Next, make the **granité au Vouvray pétillant**. Boil the water and sugar together, then leave to cool. Add the Vouvray. Pour the liquid into a* *shallow container and put it into the freezer. Once it has hardened and you are ready to serve it, scrape it with a fork to make little crystals. Place the crystals on a plate and serve the Crémets d'Anjou with a few prunes on top.*

touring around

It would be better not to read before lunch about the punishment meted out to the conspirators of the *conjuration d'Amboise*, but if you're going to visit the château in the morning, it's inevitable that you'll hear about it. Rest assured that you're unlikely to be sprung upon by a band of 500 *cavaliers* while you're having lunch at Noizay.

French royalty is still alive and well and it owns the **Château d'Amboise** (*open July and Aug, 9–8; April–June, 9–6.30; Sept and Oct, 9–6; Feb, March and Nov, 9–12 and 2–5.30; Dec and Jan, 9–12 and 2–5*), under the guise of the Fondation St-Louis. Its head, Monseigneur le comte de Paris, is a descendant of the Orléans branch of the royal family and of Louis Philippe, king from 1830 to 1848, 1848 being another French revolutionary year, one in which Louis Philippe was forced to flee to Britain under the subtle pseudonym of 'Mr Smith'! The royal presence at Amboise is discreet nowadays, but at one stage in French history the château became an animated centre of royal life. The many sides of the complex of buildings that was erected on Amboise's upper plateau during the 15th and 16th centuries have for the most part disappeared. However, the remnants are still substantial and the tour is made interesting by the fine furnishings within and a care for detail. The place was heavily restored in the last century, after the royal branch of the house of Orléans regained this royal seat in 1873.

Charles VII was the first royal to own the place. He and his son, Louis XI, did develop the castle substantially, although virtually nothing remains from their times. Louis XI established the knightly order of St-Michel here in 1469. It was during Charles VIII's time, however, that the Château d'Amboise became the centre of the kingdom. Charles, son of Louis XI, spent his cosseted childhood here and loved it, so he decided to lavish money on the castle's expansion when he became king. The new building campaign at Amboise began in 1492. The heavily restored wing overlooking the Loire, flanked on one side by the monster Tour des Minimes, and the equally massive Tour

Heurtault overlooking the Amasse valley, remain. All that still stands of the most westerly parts of the château apart from the fortified walls is the beautiful Chapelle St-Hubert. This jewel-box chapel with its needle of a spire sits precariously on the edge of the fortifications. It's a glorious work of late Gothic. It's also supposed to contain the bones of Leonardo da Vinci, who died in Amboise in 1519, having been called over to serve François I in the last years of his life.

Charles VIII had accidentally bumped his head at the château in 1498 and promptly died. His successor Louis XII moved to Blois, but the man to succeed him, François I, was brought up here in part, and made the place the centre of many extravagant royal celebrations. And later, the children of his son Henri II and of Catherine de' Medici spent much of their upbringing in the healthy Loire air here. But the atmosphere was shattered by the Wars of Religion.

The *conjuration d'Amboise* might be described as France's much earlier foreshadowing of England's Gunpowder Plot, but in reverse. In this case, Huguenots plotted in 1560 to overthrow the controlling ultra-Catholic de Guises. Initially, the capture of the de Guises was to take place at the Château de Blois. But La Renaudie, recruiting officer for the Huguenots, was indiscreet and confided the date to des Avenelles, a Paris lawyer who let the cat slip out of the bag. An extraordinary period of paranoia ensued.

The king, the young and sickly François II, married to Mary, Queen of Scots, had been out hunting with the court around the Loire. It was decided to retreat to the strong defences of Amboise. The Huguenots planned a second attack, but again a defector warned the Catholic side and divulged that many of the conspirators were gathering at the Château de Noizay. This time the de Guise faction set out with a 500-strong cavalry division. The little château was surrounded and the conspirators taken. On news of this blow, La Renaudie acted rashly. He ordered the scattered rebel troops to converge on Amboise, but without giving them a coherent plan of action. Arriving in dribs and drabs, they were easily caught. From this moment on the blood would really flow throughout France. In fanatical Catholic fashion, the de Guises had an unhealthy lust for the stuff. Executions followed in nauseating waves at Amboise. The most famous image of the suppression of the Huguenots at Amboise is of bodies left to hang from the château's battlements and from the iron rails of the balcony over-looking the Loire. Other conspirators were tied up in sacks and thrown into the river to drown.

After this appalling period the Château d'Amboise was more or less abandoned by royalty until the 19th century. In the 18th century, attention switched to the grand new Château de Chanteloup which the duc de Choiseul, a national figure of prime importance under Louis XV, had built outside the town. The **Pagode de Chanteloup** (*open July and Aug, 9.30–8; June, 10–7; Mar–May and Sept–15 Nov, 10–6; 17–28 Feb, 2–5*), 2.5km south of Amboise via the D31, is the enchanting, slightly sadly comical remnant of the great Château de Chanteloup. The pagoda's seven decreasing circles end with a clownish hat of lead topped by a golden ball. An architectural Pierrot, the form is reflected in a semi-circular pool, a lake *en demi-lune*.

Around lunchtime you could go for a short wander around the **Château de Noizay's** grounds. The place has several interesting corners, including its troglodyte caves and its wood with animal statues. Or the château can supply a little leaflet giving precise details of a walking tour of the village. It suggests visiting the church and going past the Château de Monaville, as well as the Manoir du Grand Coteau, where the great 20th-century composer Francis Poulenc once lived. Noizay lies in the region producing Vouvray wines. A good Noizay *viticulteur* to visit would be Claude Moine. He is based close to the château—ask for directions. As well as having his wine cellar in the rock, he makes good wine and is quite a local figure.

With just the afternoon in **Tours**, head first for the graceful Renaissance towers of the cathedral topping the imposing and slightly wonky Gothic building. Inside, admire the stained glass of the choir and transepts and look at the sad and beautiful tomb of Charles VIII and Anne de Bretagne's children. The former archbishop's palace next to the cathedral has been transformed into the city's fine arts museum. At least go in through the gates to appreciate the grounds and the stuffed elephant in one of the outbuildings.

Head just a little north of the cathedral square and turn left along the rue Colbert as far as the Eglise St-Julien area. Old cake preserved for posterity counts among other truly bizarre exhibits in the **Musée du Compagnonnage** (*open every day except Tues: mid-June–mid-Sept,*

9–6.30; April–mid-June, 9–12 and 2–6; rest of year 9–12 and 2–5) in the former 16th-century dormitory houses of the abbey of St-Julien. This is surely the strangest museum along the Loire. It's crammed with craftsmen's chefs-d'œuvre, made with all the pride of their various professions, the pieces executed for their own sakes rather than for a practical purpose, on a miniature scale for most, although the *pâtissiers* have been given free rein to produce monster-sized gâteaux. In its confused way the museum celebrates the artistry of the finest French craftsmen, with hocus-pocus about medieval trade guilds thrown in.

Cross the rue Nationale in front of St-Julien, maybe going up to the river to take a look at Tours' once-great trading quays, and then head west to the place Plumereau, social hub of Tours, via the rue de Commerce. The **Musée du Gemmail** (*open April–mid-Oct, Tues–Sun, 10–12 and 2–6.30. Closed Mon, except when public hol: take the rue Briçonnet from the square and then turn into rue du Mûrier*) is another of Tours's very unusual museums, celebrating a radiant contemporary development in the art of stained glass, layer upon layer of which is superimposed to create a deeply luminous picture. The term *gemmail* was coined by Jean Cocteau, one of the many notable artists to rave about this stained-glass art form. It derives from the amalgamation of the words *gemme* and *émail* (enamel) and doesn't refer to gems, but to coloured glass. This process of interpretation may sound as though it would give rather brash results, but all the painters whose works have been interpreted in this manner have seemingly been quite ecstatic, including Picasso and Braque.

You could go back to the timberframed façades of the place Plumereau and to one of the cafés to lounge and watch Tours's beautiful people go by. If you want to stay to eat in Tours, down by place Plumereau, it's not obvious how to find a good French restaurant given all the foreign and fast-food places that have taken over. The temple of cuisine in Tours is Jean Bardet's restaurant (℡ 02 47 41 41 11), set in a bourgeois house and gardens on the north bank of the river, up from the main stone bridge, the Pont Wilson. Jean Bardet is one of the most famous chefs in France. It turns out that the chef at the Château de Noizay, Didier Frébou, was previously second in command at Jean Bardet!

Maryse's Feast in the Loir Valley

La Possonnière.

The Loir (without an 'e') valley—a microcosm of the Loire valley, for travellers from Britain a precursor of the latter as you speed south, an echo of it as you trudge back up north—is tempting for a first or final stop when crossing through western France. And there's no better place to plump for along the Loir's length than the hillside village of Troo.

The Loir valley lies in tufa limestone territory like the Loire, the light, bright stone characterizing the houses here too. And along with tufa quarrying in the region come the inevitable troglodyte caves. Troo is riddled with them. In fact, the very name apparently derives from the French word for a hole, *trou*. Are the locals pulling your leg when they claim that the idiosyncratic spelling of the village name comes from an attempt to put down in writing the way the English troops may have pronounced the place when they passed through in the Middle Ages?

The Loir's beauty was sung by France's greatest lyric poet, the Loir-born Pierre de Ronsard. He was, with Rabelais, the finest of France's 16th-century Renaissance writers. Ronsard's romantic verse flows like a river. You can visit the Ronsards' Loir manor house, the Manoir de la Possonnière, just a few kilometres from Troo. The house itself is actually covered with quotes incised in the stone, and its hillside contains a string of caves that once housed passing pilgrims. The Château de Poncé is another discreet aristocratic house near Troo. It hides against the Loir hillside in a village packed with artisans.

It's hard to convey the tranquil beauty of this stretch of the Loir valley in words. Troo looks out onto a landscape of what you might imagine romantically to be an almost medieval beauty. From the grassy knoll at the top of the village, the remnants of an early medieval fort, you look down onto the fertile expanse of the valley and the tiny helmeted church of St-Jacques-des-Guérets. Venture through its cemetery and you'll discover the beauty and power of Romanesque painting. Another medieval village nearby to the east, whose castle ruins would have made a German Romantic landscape painter swoon, is Lavardin.

getting there

We'd like to insist that you approach Troo from the south. Get onto the little D10 on the lower bank of the Loir river, coming either from Montoire or from La Chartre. Turn north for Troo when you reach the D8. Approaching it this way from the flat valley plain, you get the most beautiful of views onto this lovely hillside village with its pudding-shaped, grassed-over fortress at the top. You want to head for the heights for Le Petit Relais.

To do this, once you've crossed the river, turn westwards out of the lower village. Just a little way outside it, keep your eyes peeled for the sign marked to the *cité troglodyte* and the *collégiale*. In the upper village, the restaurant is close to the entrance to the collegiate church. In motorway terms, Troo is very roughly equidistant between the A10 (exit for Château-Renault) and the A11 (exit for Vibraye).

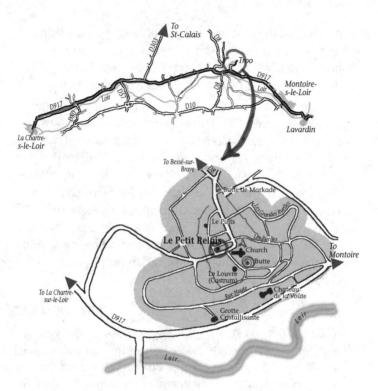

Le Petit Relais

*Le Petit Relais, 41800 Troo, © 02 54 72 57 92. Closed Mon lunchtime. Plat
du jour 50F. For 3 courses count on between 150F and 180F.*

From the outside, Le Petit Relais looks like an unassuming, neat village
house, in clean-cut bright beige blocks of Loir stone, with simple windows and a small sign for the place sticking out from a wisteria-
covered corner. A very narrow slice of terrace in front of the house
allows room for just a couple of small tables in summer. You need to
enter the dining room to savour the full atmosphere of the place.

The beamed room welcomes you with the warmth of a fireplace on
one side, logs stacked up beside it even in the height of summer. A
homely *buffet* stands on the other side of the room, apéritif bottles
lined up on that. The walls within, rather than being in the carefully

cut stone of the façade, are of smaller stone cemented together by a warm orangey-coloured filling. Pink paper tablecloths are placed over green linen cloths, matching the pink paint between the beams.

The tables will doubtless have been lovingly set with candles in petal-shaped holders, pink and white sugared almonds, and fresh seasonal flowers. Dark-stemmed wine glasses and terracotta wine coolers wait to be filled. Wine bottles have been laid down in various places around the room, some by the fireplace, some even under it in summer. The rustic feel of the place is added to by the collection of old cooking utensils.

The homely kitchen lies just off the dining room. It's clearly visible behind the bar with mock gargoyles plonked on top. You may just possibly hear Maryse Denglehem talking to herself. A harsh critic of her own cooking, sometimes she may not be quite satisfied enough; at others she may be giving herself a little encouragement. She explains that she needs to tell herself from time to time '*Et bien ma vieille, c'est pas si mal que ça.* (Well my old dear, it's not that bad.)'!

The cookery at Le Petit Relais is a one-woman show. Born of French peasant stock, Maryse can remember her early days watching the adults working on a chicory farm up north and going to help out. She calls cooking *un jeu d'enfant*, child's play, and explains that as the oldest child of a large family, she learnt to cook from the age of six when her mother fell ill. Her father was amazed at the way she took to the task. But even with that upbringing she doesn't treat cooking as a chore now, rather as a creative exercise, even if as lone potato peeler at Le Petit Relais she can get sick of some of the labour involved. Maryse has lived in the Vendômois for over 30 years and worked selling wine for 20 years, but she has only realized her ambition of running a restaurant since her mid fifties and the mid-1990s. She inherited the name of Le Petit Relais when she took the place on. The main markets where she does her shopping are the ones held at Montoire, on Wednesdays and Saturdays. She highly recommends them—they're *épatant*, brilliant, as she puts it. '*Je m'inspire des produits du marché,*' she adds.

The number of choices on the menu isn't wide. You can either opt for a *plat du jour* (50F) or choose from the homemade menu, decorated with drawings of flowers, written in slightly wonky hand. Remember the film *Babette's Feast*? That showed a Catholic outsider bringing a little lightness and even good cheer to an austere Danish community through her inspired cooking of a banquet for the community. Le Petit Relais may look fairly simple and rustic, but to any dour Protestants visiting, they might see the owner's cooking as that of Catholic temptation and excess. The style is unrepentantly French traditional— tasty, copious, rich, pampering.

The meal might start with big slices of country pâté served on a bed of lettuce with a tomato cut in the shape of a flower. *Tête de veau*, veal brawn, is a local speciality that may crop up from time to time. Or you might try the more friendly sounding *capilotade de lapin*, an aromatic rabbit dish. Snails feature regularly, for example with a garlic butter and mushrooms. The main courses incorporate many local products. The *jambon sarthois*, ham from the *département* of the Sarthe, through which the Loir flows just west of Troo, came with well flavoured creamy spinach. *Andouillette* might come in a local Loir vin de Jasnières sauce. With the extravagant *tournedos châtelain*, steak prepared with foie gras and a peppr sauce. The cockerel was served on a bed of wheat, done as a delicious risotto.

Fish regulars include eels and *sandre*, the pikeperch often mixed as a *panaché* with perch, *brochet*. *Brochet* by itself might be prepared in the fashion given below. The orange butter sauce not only imparts flavour to the fish but also acts as an excellent tangy accompaniment to the asparagus. Once again, as on the Loire's alluvial sands, the Loir valley bed is excellent for growing vegetables of all kinds. Coming to Troo from the south you may have seen fields full of vegetables. The last time we went, little salads had been planted there in vast numbers.

Some of the dishes Maryse enjoys making are marathons of prepartion. The *gigot de sept heures*, otherwise known as *gigot à la cuiller*, is one of her favourites. The lamb is left to cook in Coteaux du Layon, a well-regarded sweet Anjou white, spiced with garlic and herbs, for up to seven hours. After such a long tenderization, the lamb should be so soft that it should be possible to eat the meat with a spoon, hence the name *à la cuiller*. She also prepares lots of dishes using not just Loire valley, but Loir valley wines as well.

It would be an excellent idea to try one of these local wines with your meal. They are good value. There's a little selection of Coteaux du Vendômois whites. Jasnières can produce sweet wines from so-called noble rot; you'll find this kind listed under the *moelleux* list. Save that type for an apéritif or a dessert if you want to try it. Otherwise there is the drier Jasnières white on offer.

In summer, Maryse might have got strawberries from the market to prepare her *feuillantine aux fraises* pudding. Or local apples may be used in a *chaud-froid de pommes*. The *étoilée exotique* employs less French fruit, served in a butter sauce. As to lovers of the exotic cocoa bean, you should be well pleased with the *gâteau des prélats*, decadent enough for a cardinal, a *gênoise* coffee sponge in a chocolate ganache.

Brochet au Beurre d'Orange et Asperges Vertes

Serves 4

1 litre/1 ¾ pints water
1 carrot, sliced
1 onion, sliced
1 celery stick, chopped
1 tablespoon lemon juice
few sprigs parsley
1 bay leaf
3 or 4 black peppercorns
2 teaspoons salt
800g/1 ¾ lbs pike or mackerel fillets
750ml/1 ¼ pints single cream
5 oranges
200g/7oz butter
1kg/2lbs 4oz asparagus
1 ½ tablespoons crushed peppercorns, to garnish

First, make a court-bouillon. Put the water, carrot, onion, celery stick, lemon juice, sprigs of parsley, bay leaf, peppercorns and salt into a saucepan, bring to the boil, then cover and simmer gently for 30 minutes. Cook the fish in the court-bouillon for 6–7 minutes.

Meanwhile, heat the cream and cook, stirring, so it reduces and thickens a little. Squeeze the juice from 3 of the oranges and add this to the cream. Season to taste with salt and pepper. Place the pan over another half full of simmering water, the whisk the butter into the sauce to thicken it.

Cook the asparagus until just tender. Place the fish on a serving plate, cover with the creamy orange sauce, then garnish with the crushed peppercorns and slices of the remaining 2 oranges. Serve with the asparagus.

---

touring around

Lavardin, very close to the market town of Montoire, has a ruined castle on a hillside worthy of a German Romantic painting. The picture-book village also boasts a church which contains a full collection of wall paintings. The pretty houses climbing the bank above the meander of the river make the place altogether worthy of its rosette as a member of the association of *Les plus beaux villages de France*.

The church in the valley on the southern side of the Loir from **Troo** is **St-Jacques-des-Guérets**, a delightful, clumsy Romanesque box inside, painted with very fine Romanesque art. You have to go through a typical French cemetery with its fake flower mementoes and photos of the dead to enter the simple building. Along with familiar New Testament scenes, look out for a couple of symbolic depictions of sins—the over-proud knight falling from his horse, the lustful woman piercing her breast. One panel illustrates a part of the life of St Nicholas. The story goes that St Nicholas generously helped out a pauper with three daughters to marry off by throwing three bags of gold into the desperate man's house. Nicholas is of course the saint whose generosity we tend to celebrate not on his feast day of 6 December, but on 25 December.

Do take the time before lunch to amble around the now generally very peaceful **upper village of Troo**, small sections of its defensive walls preserved. The Louvre here was a fortified castle built for the counts of Anjou and later fought over by Richard the Lionheart and Philippe Auguste in the clash between Plantagenets and Capetians which so marked the valley. You may stumble across the *puits qui parle*, the talking well with its echoing depths. You should certainly climb up the snailing path of the rounded mound, a medieval *motte*. From up top you get the most splendid views imaginable onto the Loir valley, an exhilarating sight to savour over the meal. You could also take a look into the sturdy old Romanesque-to-Gothic collegiate church dedicated to St Martin. From close by the church, take a track down into the hillside troglodyte village. Troo's cliff is filled with private dwellings, caverns in the rock turned into houses. You can get glimpses into some of the troglodyte homes. There is one house done up in the old-fashioned way and open to visitors.

After lunch, go a little west from Troo to Couture-sur-Loir and the **Manoir de la Possonnière** (*guided tours 16 June–Aug, Wed–Sun and public hols at 3.30, 4.30 and 5.30 on the dot: same times for rest of opening period, between Apr–1 Nov, but only Sat, Sun and public hols*) where the poet Ronsard was born. The Renaissance is written all over this house, literally—the windows of La Possonnière are graced with Latin inscriptions on good living, set in the splendid local yellow-golden stone. Many of these adornments were added in 1515 by Loys Ronsard, Pierre the poet's father, in celebration of his marriage—a fine and lasting way to mark the occasion.

Exciting the curiosity, in the hillside diagonally opposite this Gothic–Renaissance manor, an extraordinary row of entrances, again with inscriptions over each of the doorways, give into the rock. The words above the seven caves signal the purposes of the different chambers. The manor house was a stopping point on a pilgrimage route and many travellers could rest here. '*Sustine et abstine*' exhorts you to 'sustenance and abstinence' in the kitchen, while the '*custodia dapum*' indicates the food store. '*Cui des videto*', 'look to whom you give', was a reception room for travellers. The '*vina barbara*' refers to the wine cellar, '*vulcano et diligentiae*' to the smithy (horses were guests too of course), while '*la fovriere*' held the hay and '*la buanderie belle*' was where clothes were washed. You can visit the substantial kitchen cave. The marks at the end show how this was a former quarry and the method by which the stone was extracted. During the guided tour the humorous inscriptions on the manor house and the rich symbols on the main family fireplace are also explained.

The Loir passes from the Loir-et-Cher into the neighbouring *département* of the Sarthe after Couture. **Poncé** is an animated little village just beyond the border, invaded by craftspeople who have settled along its main street. The crafts activity is limited to the lower village. You could head for the Centre d'Art et d'Artisanat in 18th-century mill buildings by the Loir. Signs show jewellers, glassblowers, potters and cabinetmakers among the many craftspeople at work. A hat maker, a weaver and a candle-maker count among the other traders. You can pay to go on a guided tour during which you'll see several crafts in action. Outside the centre, you can also wander into a number of other craft shops along the main road, with painted furniture, lace and antique clothes among their attractions.

The **Château de Poncé** (*open April–Sept, 10–12—except Sun am—and 2–6*) has known more elegant days. Its grounds used to stretch handsomely down to the Loir. Now the remaining garden and the château have been cruelly separated from it by the busy road from which a wall protects it, while a 19th-century monstrosity has marred the cliff face behind it. The entrance via the outbuildings isn't the most enticing, but once into the grounds you should be pleasantly surprised.

You feel almost as though you own the place as you step in through the main door, with no one to welcome or disturb you. The great staircase ascends in front of you. This is in fact the major attraction of the visit and you can take it at your own pace. Its coffered stone ceiling is filled with sculptures—136 different ones in all, apparently. Flowers, lions' heads, angels in foliage, salamanders, mythological creatures, flute-playing putti and a woman stabbing her own breast count among the panoply of Renaissance motifs. As you go up the levels, the carvings become more figurative and more fun. A bust of Ronsard stands at the top of the stairs, accompanied by a poem he wrote dedicated to the '*rivière Loir*', a humorous tale accusing his favourite river, whose praises he has so tirelessy sung, of trying to drown him when his boat capsized one day—one lesson the Renaissance apparently didn't impart to him was how to swim.

Deeply Dappled Shade in the Forêt de Bercé

L'Hermitière

The forest of Bercé provides deeply dappled shade below its soaring oaks in the height of summer. Its woods lie just north of the Loir valley, on a horseshoe-shaped plateau that stretches up from La Chartre-sur-le-Loir, bends round above the village of Jupilles, and descends to Château-du-Loir. The Auberge de l'Hermitière lies in a clearing by the forest. Many people go walking or cycling in the woods, for example to visit one of the great oaks dating back several centuries. At Jupilles there's even a little *musée du bois*, a museum in a wood.

We're now in the very southern section of the *département* of the Sarthe. It's here, just below the Forêt de Bercé, that the Loir slopes provide the territory for the best Loir wines. Head west along the gentle valley and once through the fruit-growing territory of Vaas you come to Le Lude, dominated by the most grandiose château on the Loir.

getting there

The Sources de L'Hermitière close to which you'll find the restaurant lie on the eastern edge of the forest. From La Chartre follow the D304 northwestwards, passing through St-Pierre-du-Lorouër (c.10km). After St-Pierre-du-Lorouër watch out for a turning to the left, a little before St-Vincent-du-Lorouër (a further 3.5km along the road). The signs in the forest have been made from wood, but this means that they're quite hard to spot, so slow down for them. You turn onto a deeply wooded, branch-vaulted forest road and at the bottom of a steep dip turn for L'Hermitière. Once past the public picnic spots, as you arrive at the inn you emerge back into the light. If you're travelling through western France by motorway and wish to reach the restaurant, it's roughly midway between the A10 (exit north of Tours) and the A11 (exit east of Le Mans).

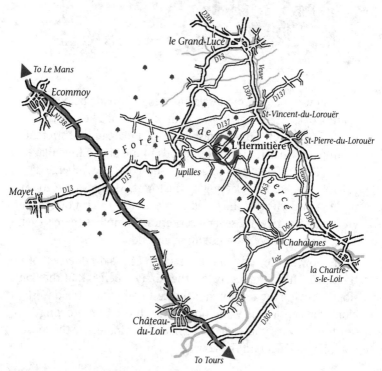

Deeply Dappled Shade in the Forêt de Bercé

L'Auberge de l'Hermitière

L'Auberge de l'Hermitière, 72150 St-Vincent-du-Lorouër, © 02 43 44 84 45, ✆ 02 43 79 10 04. Closed Mon evenings and Tues, and from the beginning of Nov to the middle of March. Menus at 85F (weekdays only), 140F, 155F and 195F.

The Virginia creeper on the front of this inn conceals what isn't the prettiest of façades, but the plant turns particularly beautiful colours in autumn. The restaurant front is broken up by wide windows with brick surrounds. Apparently the building, from the 1950s, was made to store railway tracks originally. Flower boxes bring touches of brightness to the upper windows and there's a barn attached to the house. On the opposite side of the quiet road in front of the restaurant, a little terrace has room for a good nine or ten tables, with some trees planted among the set-white gravel squares. You can look down from the terrace on to a small liver-shaped lake, its waters not murky enough to hide the carp swimming around it. Little white fencing with a row of roses adds an oddly civilized touch.

Cyclists, rather than cars, drew up when we ate at the *auberge*. The Hermitière is the name of the stream that rises here, but there are two conflicting theories as to how it got this name. The pure one is that a hermit, St Fraimbault, came to settle here. Another says that the name may not be so innocent and that this was a place where women came to do their washing…only that wasn't all a few came for. Apparently the word '*ermite*' can be a euphemism for a woman of loose morals.

We ate outside, but it's worth casting an eye in at the dining room. This is extremely curious rather than immediately charming, but becomes more and more amusing as you observe the details. The most striking and bizarre element is the tree trunk rising up through the middle of it! It disappears into a large piece of linen draped over the room, like a great tablecloth hiding the ceiling. The massive trunk is that of a pear tree, reckoned to be some 400 years old. That would mean it could possibly date from King Henri IV's time.

The pear tree is a lot older than the most distinguished guest to have graced the restaurant with her presence, no less a figure than the British Queen Mother, who came here in 1984, while she was visiting the Château du Lude. The chef-cum-proprietor had already done England the honour of not just visiting it, but also working there a while, including a small stint with the Roux brothers at the Waterside Inn. Guy Podevin is this restaurateur's wonderfully fitting name. (A *pot de vin* means not just a jug of wine in French, but also a bribe!) Guy Podevin is also a sculptor. No prizes for guessing his favoured medium—wood. A few of his extremely smoothly finished works are displayed in the dining room. He and his wife have been here over 20 years. The experience doesn't appear to have aged them. His many occupations extend well beyond his restaurant—he is a local mayor and president of the Loir restaurant association, the Bonnes Etapes.

On to M. Podevin's other art. There were menus at 140F and 155F, but this is one of those rare restaurants where it might be worth choosing *à la carte* as the prices aren't that exorbitant. While we were choosing we decided to try a local wine by way of apéritif. The waiter may well suggest a Jasnières as a refreshing sweet apéritif, for example the Cuvée Louise 1995 *vendange tardive*, the grapes probably picked on hazy late autumn days when the noble rot sets in. This was surprisingly good. Alternatively, you might be adventurous and celebratory, and try the Gigou Pétillant du Loir, Blanc de Blanc, a local sparkling wine. *Le cocktail de l'Hermite*, though, is *crème de mûre* mixed with cider—well, it makes a change from blackberry and apple pie. The cocktail is a reminder that north of the Loir, wine country disappears to give way to cider country. We are here on the frontier of the old French province of Maine, just below Normandy. As we sipped our Jasnières, beyond our conversation, bird song, cooking pans rattling and chatter in the kitchen were the only sounds we could make out.

'*Des bases très terroir, avec une pointe de fantaisie* (Very much based around local tradition, with a little bit of my own imagination thrown in)' is the way Guy Podevin describes his cooking. He also explains that he is '*assez saucier*', which doesn't mean that he's quite saucy, but that he rather likes making sauces. No bad thing as sauces are the truly great element in French cuisine. He learnt many tricks from working with an old chef who'd mastered his art at the Paris Ritz and the Savoy. The *menu plaisir* is a simple combination, a seasonal salad followed by a main course chosen *à la carte* and the day's pudding. We concentrated on the *menu vallée du Loir*, four courses for 155F. *Andouillettes* are popular across France and a bit of a speciality here, so you could try them warm in a salad as a starter. Those wishing to stick closer to vegetables could go for a mixed salad of *crudités*. The rich *terrine campagnarde* was made with chicken livers. You may find the entrées *à la carte* more exciting and original. The *pot au feu de canard et foie gras* was an excellent duck stew, set in a Chenin Blanc (a grape variety) jelly and served chilled. Or most appropriately you could go for the much simpler but delicious warm *champignons sylvestres*, wild mushrooms from the forest. There were *pieds bleu*, *pholiotes* (delicious, noticeable little black mushrooms) and some ceps and *girolles*, served with mixed grains and salad leaves. An excellent forest starter.

The main courses on the *menu vallée du Loir* include a *sauté sarthois*, Guy Podevin's version of the classic Sarthe dish, the *marmite sarthoise*. The *marmite* normally mixes rabbit meat with chicken. Guy Podevin has replaced the rabbit with snails, believing that chicken and snails go excellently together. And they do, especially with Jasnières wine and cream added in the sauce. You might also have been very tempted by the *rognon de porc au cidre*, pork kidneys in cider, a dish which won Guy Podevin a national cookery prize. Other interesting *plats de résistance à la carte* include the young pigeon whose recipe is given below, prized Loué chicken breasts served with mushrooms, and *sandre* in Jasnières.

Cow's milk cheese features more here than goat's milk cheese. There was Petit Troo from so close by, while the Vendômois is aged *sur place*. We drank a Coteaux du Loir Pineau d'Aunis with our meal. This grape variety is normally mixed with Gamay, so it's a rarity of the Loir to find it vinified by itself. It was very light and cherryish, with a slight peppery flavour. You could also try a local wine simply made from Côt, the same grape variety that's so popular in Cahors. Here it doesn't make such tannic wine, but is lighter and fruity, with those hints generally described as of *sous bois*, undergrowth. Perhaps you could go round sniffing the forest floor afterwards to test out whether you agree.

To cool us in summer, the first pudding proposed on the list, the *neige d'été et fruits frais compoté au vin du Loir* sounded too tempting to resist. Refreshing and slightly heady. The *neige* is a *granité*, ice flavoured with a sweet white wine and syrup, and then grated into little pieces. Or again following the woodland theme, you could go for a forest fruits *coulis* accompanying ice-cream as well as the grilled almonds and local forest honey. We couldn't help noticing that the delicious *pêches en chemise croustillante, sauce cachou* was a bit risqué, seemingly influenced by French adverts, which always, but always have to show women's breasts. The peaches were all too clearly popping out of their very light biscuit blouse.

Pigeonneau du Pays de Racan Mariné en Bécassine

When choosing fresh pigeon, good signs are small eyes, soft red feet, short rounded spurs, bright neck feathers the same colour as the body and a soft beak. They need to be plucked, drawn, singed and washed like a chicken, except that the feet are left on, simply dipped in boiling water and scraped.

Serves 4

4 young pigeons (squab) of 300–400g each
3 shallots, chopped
1 carrot, sliced
200g/7oz fresh chanterelle mushrooms (or other fresh wild mushrooms)
12 baby carrots
four sprigs each fresh thyme
3 bay leaves
handful juniper berries
500ml/17fl oz red Coteaux du Loir
250ml/8fl oz chicken stock
50g/2oz butter
2 tablespoons oil

Marinate the pigeons overnight with the bones in the red wine, to which you have added the shallots (reserving about 1 tablespoon), carrot, thyme, bay leaves and juniper berries.

The next day, transfer the bones and the marinade to a saucepan, pour in the stock and simmer for 30 minutes. Then, pour the sauce through a chinois (a conical strainer) into a clean pan. Let it simmer and reduce by a little over a third, until it is a good gravy consistency, then keep warm on one side. Preheat the oven to 220°C/425°F (gas mark 7).

Next, prepare the vegetables. Blanch the baby carrots, plunging them into boiling water for about 1 minute, then sauté them in half of the butter until tender and glossy. Sauté the chanterelles in a third of the butter together with the reserved shallots.

Meanwhile, fry the pigeons briskly, skin side down, in the oil. Turn them over and fry briefly. Place them on a lightly greased baking sheet and bake them for a few minutes in the preheated oven. Make sure they remain pink.

Reheat the sauce, whisking in the remaining butter until it has all been incorporated and the sauce is a good consistency and is beautifully glossy. Carve the pigeons into escalopes. Fan the escalopes out on the warmed serving plates. Add the vegetable accompaniments and ladle the sauce over them and around the pigeon.

---

touring around

The most venerated trees in the **Forêt de Bercé** stand in the *futaie des clos*, a short distance southeast of the Sources de l'Hermitière, with its three most venerated old trunks, the Chêne Boppe, the Nouveau Chêne Boppe and the Chêne Roulleau among eight hectares of centuries-old trees. The last two of these massive oaks are accorded three stars in the French Guide Bleu, so highly is their cultural stature considered! They are around 300 years old, planted under Louis XIV. Nature lovers come to worship them, although the original Chêne Boppe was unfortunately severely truncated by a lightning strike in 1935. You can enjoy a good wander through the forest.

Jupilles has a little museum, the Maison du Sabot et de l'Artisanat du Bois (*open Easter to All Saints, 2.30–6.30, but closed Mon*), devoted to wood and its professions. It isn't so much lumberjacks, charcoal-burners, turners or cabinetmakers who are celebrated in the place, but the *sabotiers*, the clogmakers. At one time Jupilles was overcrowded with 400 of them. At the start of this century they were producing more than 400,000 pairs a year, some for export to Holland! Now the practical craft remembered here has all but died out. However, a number of local enterprises have tried to keep alive old traditions, producing and selling wooden objects and toys as well as leather.

Rejoin the Loir at La Chartre, a pretty little town. Just east of it, towards Poncé, are **Lhomme** and **Ruillé**, the two villages most closely associated with winemaking in the Loir valley. At Lhomme, a small Musée de la Vigne is open in July and August (*3–6pm, except Mon*). The Coteau de Jasnières is signposted at Ruillé, a small patch of slopes with fine views over the valley producing the highest quality Loir wine from the Chenin Blanc grape variety.

West of La Chartre, head for Marçon, then past the Lac de Varenne to cross back north of the Loir close to Le Port Gautier. Continue along the valley past Château-du-Loir and Vaas, an area of fruit orchards. **Le Lude** is our main destination for the afternoon. The Château du Lude (*open Apr–Sept: gardens 10–12 and 2–6; house 2.30–6*) is without a doubt the most famous château on the Loir, probably thought by many French people to be on the Loire in fact. It fits in with the monster châteaux there. Each of its corners is marked by a massive round tower. The towers are covered with Renaissance decoration, showing that, yes, we have another great Gothic-to-Renaissance transitional château. Actually, the architecture here extends over many centuries, with bits and pieces from the 13th to the 18th. Apart from its Renaissance aspects, though, the château's other major outer features are the 18th-century alterations. These have given the inner courtyard the metropolitan feel of a great town house, while a massive classical east front has been packed in tightly between the two towers on that side. This is the great façade reflected in the Loir, particularly spectacularly during the summer night *son-et-lumière*. A great balustraded terrace runs above the river from the south wing, part of the spacious gardens which stretch out on this side, whereas the north and west sides are shoved up against the town. The château was largely rebuilt after serving as a stronghold in the second part of the Hundred Years War, guarding as it did an important river crossing. The interiors are mainly stamped by 18th- and 19th-century living in particular. But the 16th-century interior decoration must have been splendid, to go by the one little painted cabinet that has survived from that time.

Spoilt for Choice: the Indre and Châteaux West of Tours

Azay-le-Rideau

Azay-le-Rideau—in France the name rolls off the tongue as familiarly as Chambord and Chenonceau. Azay-le-Rideau resembles the latter in that its gorgeous form is reflected in water. Rather than the Cher river, here it is the Indre on which this swan of a building is reflected. And while Chenonceau lies in eastern Touraine, Azay-le-Rideau is in the west, well situated for a posse of further famous châteaux nearby: Villandry (at the end of the Cher), with its fabulous vegetable gardens, Langeais on the Loire, its stern exterior hiding a tapestry-warmed interior, and Ussé (further down the Indre), the château that inspired Perrault's tale, *La Belle au bois dormant*, more familiarly known to us in English as *Sleeping Beauty*. In short, Azay-le-Rideau is at the centre of an area which turns out to be one of the most densely châteaued corners in France. We'd suggest three château courses for the day: the fabulous vegetable gardens of Villandry as the entrée, Azay-le-Rideau for the main course and romantically sweet Ussé for pudding.

As if we weren't already spoilt for choice on the cultural menu, this is also wine country. The Chinon vineyards lie just south-west, while Bourgueil and St-Nicolas-de-Bourgueil are bottled just north over the Loire. But Azay has its own little *appellation*, Touraine-Azay-le-Rideau, its wines a cut above your average Touraine. In spring the area immediately surrounding Azay also blossoms with innumerable lines of fruit trees which produce apples and pears in huge numbers in the autumn.

getting there

Coming off the A10 motorway you need to take the exit south of Tours, marked for Chambray. Follow the signs for Montbazon, then Monts, and continue along the Indre via Saché to Azay-le-Rideau. If you're coming from the south you could take the more southerly motorway exit for Ste-Maure-de-Touraine and briefly follow the D760 to Noyant before turning there for the D57 via St-Epain and Villaines-les-Rochers up to Azay-le-Rideau.

If you're arriving from the centre of Tours, you can take the busy commercial N10 south as far as Montbazon to then enjoy the nicer Indre route west. However, the most secretive and wonderful way from Tours is to head west along the southern bank of the Loire from the centre of town (in the direction marked La Riche). Follow the isthmus *levée* road to the tip, past Berthenay, and swing round to then follow the north bank of the Cher, crossing at the village of Savonnières. This route also has the advantage of bringing you to Villandry, our first proposed stop for the day. After Villandry continue on to Azay-le-Rideau as indicated previously.

Approaching from Anjou and the west, you can choose to travel either along the north bank of the Loire, crossing south at Langeais, or along either of two routes south of the Loire, either following the great river closely by taking the D7, then joining the D17 along the Indre valley, or going via Chinon and the D751.

Note that the restaurant is in the village of La Chapelle-St-Blaise south of the river Indre, on the opposite bank to the town of Azay-le-Rideau. L'Automate Gourmand is set back at the end of a very small square-cum-car park at the junction where the D17 heads off towards Rigny-Ussé and the Château d'Ussé. A colourful *pierrot* jumps out at you from the restaurant's gabled end.

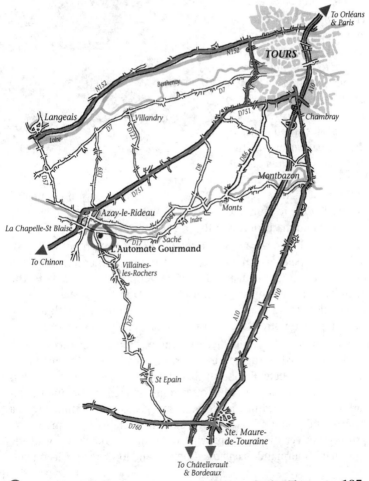

L'Automate Gourmand

*L'Automate Gourmand, 1 rue du Parc, La
Chapelle-St-Blaise, 37190 Azay-le-
Rideau, © 02 47 45 39 07. Closed
Mon eve and Tues. Closed for
hols Nov and last fortnight
Jan. Menus 65F, 87F, 137F,
148F, 188F and 248F.*

L'Avtomate Gourmand

The name of this restaurant
might confuse an English-
speaking visitor. No, an
automate gourmand isn't a
money-guzzling French
machine where you go to
get your car washed. Nor is
it some fast-food joint for
the château-rushed glutton.
Nor does the *automate* refer
to a modern faceless automaton here. It in fact makes reference to
antique mechanical puppets. A large glass cabinet covering much of
one wall of the restaurant contains a display of them. The food is anything but automatic or run of the mill, however.

While Azay-le-Rideau across the river is always packed out with visitors, La Chapelle-St-Blaise is a calm, untouristy, rather unremarkable
place. The restaurant displays its unpretentious gabled side to the
street. The French have a common expression for prospering busi-
nesses, describing them as having their *pignon sur rue*, with a gable
overhanging the street. Here it's more a case of *pignon sur parking*.

Inside, the welcome is friendly. The beamed dining room is cosy, even
slightly cramped, as the house isn't particularly large. Barely ten tables
can be fitted in here. Behind the bar you can see one of those tasteless
stuffed animals that are still so often found in French restaurant decoration. The main feature, however, is that glass cabinet, stuffed with a
bizarre and chaotic mixture of items. It contains wine maps and
posters and certificates from wine fraternities. There's a pot of the
Automate Gourmand's *confiture d'oignons* and local apple juice in bot-

tles. Among much other bric-a-brac stand the *automates* themselves, trapped inside, immobile most of the time. They include a coiffed woman grinding coffee and a figure of a chef.

The real live chef is the ultradynamic, passionate Patrice Brisacier. If he really isn't wound up hourly, then he must have unbelievable natural energy. His kitchen area lies downstairs, where there's a further simple dining room with a big fireplace. Patrice Brisacier bought the restaurant at the end of the 1980s. He had previously worked in a string of reputed restaurants, some in the Loire, including the Hosten, a good restaurant in Langeais, and the Château d'Artigny, a flash, glamorous 20th-century château down the Indre towards Montbazon.

Patrice describes his cuisine as 'classic, but when it comes to sauces, much lighter than is traditional'. He works by himself, manically, in his kitchen. His mother and girlfriend look after the customers. The menus are all generous and good value. There are three different basic ones from which you can choose. With the first, four courses can cost you under 90F. For starters, there should be a meat choice, say the very tasty beef *terrine* with tartar sauce, a seafood choice, for example a *mosaïque de la mer* (a kind of seafood *terrine*), and a vegetable option, such as a *crème de légumes*. You should get the same kind of choice with the main courses. The fish cake was definitely not your prepackaged type, extremely tasty and served with a parsley sauce. The thinly cut rumpsteak sauce came with a *sauce duxelle*, made with mushrooms and shallots sautéd in butter and cream. The vegetable option might be a *feuilleté maraîcher, œufs pochés*, Loire vegetables cooked in flaky pastry and served with poached eggs. Cheese and pudding follow.

Among the puddings you should find a delicious cake or two. Patrice's *pailletés feuillantines* we can particularly recommend. Their delicious crushiness comes from the layers of crumbs of crisp *crêpes dentelles* or *gavottes*, an extremely light Breton biscuit speciality, that he puts in. The ones we tried, one with dark chocolate, another with white chocolate, almonds and praline, were wonderful.

The puddings are the same on the next menu up, known as the *menu Rabelaisien* in the past. On this one, the four-course menu was at 148F, the five-course option at 188F. Here the homemade *confiture d'oignons* put in an appearance, served with the *marbré de lapin*. The rabbit in white wine might be cooked in a *terrine* dish lined with smoked pork. Or you could try a typically French hors d'œuvre of snails, removed from their shells and hidden under layers of flaky pastry, served with walnuts, which provide a good contrast of texture, crunchy against the softly chewy snails. The main course might be a pan-fried mousse of perch with a rich tomato sauce, or boned, stuffed quail.

On the most expensive menu, four courses cost 188F, five courses 248F. The ingredients are even more luxurious on this one. One of the finest starters is the quail salad with foie gras and quail eggs. The *terrine de foie gras de canard*, homemade, is of the best flavoured we have sampled. The *sandre* might come with a *crème de canelle*, cinnamon cream. Among the main courses was the mysterious *pot au feu d'animelles et crête de coq*. Well, we could make out that the last bit meant a rooster's crest. But *animelles*? One in the party was invited to try them. They turned up, soft little rounded balls that melted nicely in the mouth. It transpired that they were what New Zealanders euphemistically call 'mountain oysters', lamb's testicles. More proof that French cooks can make virtually all parts of an animal taste delicious—although we have yet to see sheeps' eyes on a French menu.

Terrine de Pot au Feu Fraîcheur, Sauce Tartare

You need to prepare this dish a day in advance. The secret of the success of this pot au feu fraîcheur *is that it mixes together pieces of meat with different tastes and textures; lean bits like shoulder, gelatinous bits like shin or shank and tender bits like rump.*

Serves 4

For the terrine:
250g/9oz beef shin or shank
250g/9oz beef shoulder
250g/9oz beef rump
2 carrots, finely chopped
1 onion, finely chopped

¼ celeriac

2 leeks, washed and finely chopped

bouquet garni

salt and pepper

5 leaves of gelatine or 30g/1 ¼oz powdered gelatine

1 tablespoon white or sherry vinegar

1 tablespoon gherkins, chopped

1 tablespoon capers

1 tablespoon chopped fresh parsley

1 tablespoon chopped fresh tarragon

For the tartare sauce:

1 egg yolk

10g/¼oz mustard

2 tablespoons vinegar

200ml/7fl oz groundnut oil

1 shallot, very finely chopped

1 gherkin, very finely chopped

1 teaspoon capers, finely chopped

1 teaspoon mixed fresh herbs, finely chopped (parsley and tarragon)

salt and pepper

Plunge the meat into a large pan of boiling salted water to seal it immediately so it doesn't lose any of its juices or blood. Bring back to the boil, then reduce the heat, but keep the water simmering nicely. Add the vegetables and bouquet garni. Leave to simmer gently, without a lid, for approximately 3 ½–4 hours, skimming the fat off frequently. Once the meat has cooked, drain off and reserve the stock. Break the meat up, but leave a few nice chunks so the terrine will have a good texture when you cut into it.

Return 750ml/1 ¼ pints of the stock to the pan and let it bubble away until it has reduced to about 500ml/17fl oz, then season it carefully with salt and pepper. Remove the pan from the heat and add the gelatine. Stir until it has dissolved, then add the meat, vinegar, gherkins, capers, parsley and tarragon. Pour the mixture into a large terrine or 4 ramekins. Leave to cool, then refrigerate overnight. Meanwhile, make the tartare sauce to serve with the terrine. Put the egg yolk into a bowl with the mustard, season to taste with salt and pepper, then whisk in half the vinegar until everything is well

*combined. Now, drop by drop and whisking constantly, add the oil until
you have a smooth, creamy mayonnaise. Mix in the remainder of the
vinegar slowly, and then the tartare flavourings: the gherkins, capers,
parsley and tarragon. Keep refrigerated until you are ready to serve.*

---

touring around

At the **Château de Villandry** (*open June–Sept, 9–6; Oct–mid-Nov,
9–5.30; mid-Feb–March, 9.30–5; rest of winter open during Christmas holidays only. Garden open July and Aug, 8.30am–8pm; May, June and Sept,
9–7.30; April 9–7; March and early Nov, 9–6; mid-Nov–Feb, 9–5*) vegetables are transformed into art. They are the enticing main attraction of
the château. But in truth it isn't simply the vegetables, but also the
complex geometrical and symbolic calculation of the whole ensemble
of Villandry's parterres that creates a sense of wonder and delight.
Villandry's gardens only date from the start of this century, but they re-
invent the spirit of a formal Renaissance design. They don't follow any
original plans. They were conceived by a Spanish-American couple, Dr
Joachim Carvallo and Anne Coleman who bought Villandry in 1906.
The formal French style they recreated developed out of two traditions:
the French medieval monastic garden and the Italian noble estate,
ideas on the latter brought over by the likes of Dom Pacello da
Mercogliano, one of the gifted Italians to come back with Charles VIII
from that king's forays into Italy at the close of the 15th century.
Several important elements at Villandry date from the 18th century,
such as the elevated water garden.

The famous *potager*, the kitchen or vegetable garden is surely the most
enviable kitchen garden in the world. Flowers and fruit trees have for
once to bow to the beauty of beet, the charm of comely cabbages and
lettuce, the perfection of peppers. Some of the set pieces are unforgettable: rose bushes sprouting from a dense bed of leeks, or pruned pear
trees forming the backdrop to an intense crowd of celery.

Climb the hillside to appreciate the layout of the gardens to the full.
From up here you can read clearly the symbols of love in the ornamental box hedge gardens. Fickle love takes the form of fans, objects of
dissimulation, interspersed with the horns of the cuckold, while the
love letters are apparently supposed to remind of the falsity of words

and of absence. Daggers and swords evoke the duels of tragic love. Tender love is reassuringly represented by complete hearts. In the last square, the hearts have been broken by the disruptive dance of maddened, passionate love. To the left of these interpretations of *l'amour*, various crosses and fleurs-de-lys have been cut out of further hedges. Beyond, still more represent musical symbols, with stylized lyres, harps, musical notes, and candelabra to light the sheet music.

The beauty of **Azay-le-Rideau's château** (*open July and Aug, 9–7; mid-Mar–June and Sept–Oct, 9.30–6; Nov–mid Mar, 9.30–12.30 and 2–5.30*) reflected in its moat encourages extravagant comparisons. Balzac likened it to a diamond with its multiple facets set in the Indre'. The château you see now was started in 1518 for Gilles Berthelot, a treasurer of France. Azay is so often cited as the example par excellence of French Renaissance architecture, but in fact it dates from that transitional early 16th-century period during which Gothic elements lingered on. The pepper-pot towers, the *chemin de ronde* (though not built primarily for defensive purposes), the steepness of the roof, the latter's finial tips, all give a Gothic twist to the whole. The Italian influence can be seen in the move towards symmetry, in the pilaster-framed, standardized windows, and in many of the typical Italianate decorative details. The famous staircase is renowned not just for its elaborate decoration, but also for the fact that it counts among the very first in a French château not to be housed in a protruding stair tower, but instead incorporated in the Italian manner into the main building. The emblems of the salamander and the ermine pay tribute, ironically, to the royal couple François I and Claude de France, who soon confiscated the place from the builder.

Before going inside, it's worth wandering round to the south to enjoy the splendidly broad-moated side. The château isn't reflected in the moat at all times of the year. Sometimes the water is too fast-flowing, at others it may be covered with plantlife, but when the calm waters do reflect the château's form, it makes for a memorable sight, elegant and light and sparkling. Within, the rooms are somewhat empty and unexciting, but you start the visit in the low kitchen, which has some delightful Gothic details in the *culs-de-lampe*, a hilarious dog chewing on a bone, a man mooning at visitors. After that it's the typical round of tapestries, chests and, generally speaking, bad copies of paintings. A few 16th-century royal and noble portraits are the main exception. The tapestries are particularly atmospheric in the *grande salle*, bathed in shimmering reflected light on sunny days.

Two wonderful great cedars of Lebanon stand impressively next to the many towers and turrets of the **Château d'Ussé** (*open mid-July–Aug, 9–6.30; Easter–mid July and first 3 weeks of Sept, 9–12 and 2–6.45; mid-Mar-Easter, 9–12 and 2–6; end Sept–mid-Nov, 10–12 and 2–5.30. Closed mid-Nov–mid March; adm exp*). They were a gift from the Romantic writer François René de Chateaubriand to the owner in his day, the duchesse de Duras. To the French, Ussé is a symbol of romance. The woods rise up darkly and abruptly behind its pointed roofs and windows, but the château's stone is lit a distinctive bright yellow by the sunlight, contrasting with the deep green of the foliage. It turns its back on the trees to look optimistically into the wide plain.

The tale of the tale of the writing of *Sleeping Beauty* goes that Charles Perrault, the author, stopped in the area on his way back to Paris and was put up in the château. Perrault is supposed to have been moved to pen notes here for this most famous of children's fairy tales. If you can't remember the story line exactly, you can try to piece it together from the scenes recreated with waxwork models at the top of the greatest of the château's towers. They seem to be out of sequence.

Before the guided tour around the main building, visit the separate chapel. This is a gem of an early French Renaissance building. Nuns, men with a barrel, a dog and a reptilian man with a beaded backbone count among the fine carvings on the pews, said to have come from Jean Goujon's atelier. The beautifully sweet faïence Virgin was produced by the Italian della Robbia family. Inside the château you'll find a curious hotch-potch of styles and artefacts. The best is saved until last, the *chambre du roi*. During Louis XIV's reign, leading aristocrats had to decorate one room sumptuously in case of a visit by the king. The king's room has been splendidly rejuvenated recently, with new gold-leaf detailing and rich reds framing exquisite pieces of furniture such as the Boulle bureau in red tortoise-shell and copper. Royal portraits of Louis XIV and of Mademoiselle de Blois, princesse de Conti, the daughter of the Sun King and Louise de la Vallière, add to the wealth of the room. Unfortunately the king never came.

A Pilgrimage to Candes-St-Martin, where the Vienne Meets the Loire

L'Auberge de la Route d'Or

Candes-St-Martin is a triple pilgrimage halt. This ravishing, archetypal Loire riverside village was where one of France's great saints, St Martin, died. His body was bitterly fought over by rival factions at the end of the 4th century when he passed away. A splendid church was later erected on the spot. This church also stands along one of the main routes of the pilgrimage to St James of Compostela, known as the *route d'Or*, the golden road.

The other great local pilgrimage is for fans of English royalty, to the tombs of the Plantagenet counts of Anjou who became kings of England, Henry II and Richard the Lionheart. Their tombs lie in the vast abbey of Fontevraud, along with those of Henry II's wife Eleanor of Aquitaine and King John's wife Isabelle d'Angoulême. The abbey is one of the best-preserved religious establishments in France, superbly restored for tourists since it stopped serving as a prison.

To add to all these blessings which make Candes-St-Martin such a magnetic place, from the top of the village you can get one of the finest views down onto the Loire valley, at the spot where the Vienne tributary joins it from the east. A little way back up the Vienne lies the splendid courtly town that for a short while became the headquarters of the Plantagenets, Chinon. Later the Valois took brief refuge there in the form of the dauphin, future Charles VII. It was to Chinon that Joan of Arc came all the way from Lorraine to persuade him to believe in her saints' voices directing her to help him win the Hundred Years War and boot the English out of France. In one of the most famous and most often fictionalized meetings in French history, she convinced him of her powers. Chinon remains a delicious, delightful wedge of a medieval town.

The Chinonais is well known for its red wines. And Chinon and wine are famously mixed together in some of the giant tales by locally born Rabelais, one of the great figures in French literature, a 16th-century author, doctor and intellectual.

getting there

Candes-St-Martin lies between Chinon and Saumur, on the south bank of the Loire and the Vienne where the two rivers merge. The main road through the village just manages to squeeze between the old houses and goes past the church, the focal point of the place. L'Auberge de la Route d'Or lies on the little cobbled church square. The nearest motorway exit is the Ste-Maure one on the A10. From there follow signs for Chinon and then Candes-St-Martin.

La Route d'Or

La Route d'Or, place de l'Eglise, 37500 Candes St-Martin, ℗ 02 47 95 81 10. Closed Tues pm and Wed out of season, otherwise open every day. Annual closeure 15 Nov–28 Feb, but open Christmas hols. Menus at 85F (weekdays only) 120F and 150F.

This is a hermit's cave of a restaurant, tucked into diminutive buildings by the beautiful porch entrance to the church of Candes-

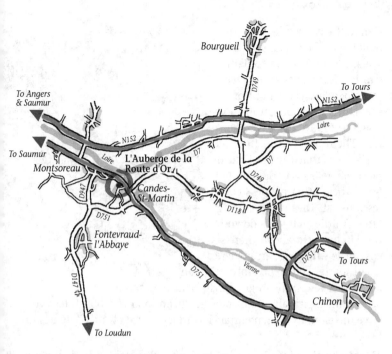

St-Martin. The **cliffsides** of the Loire and its tributaries apparently lodged many holy men in the early centuries of Christianity in France. Nowadays the hermitage-like house of the Route d'Or is for the culinary few. No coach party could possibly fit into the tiny space. In summer, tables and chairs are set out on the roughly cobbled square.

Although Candes-St-Martin has such an ancient history (St Martin died here around 1600 years ago) this restaurant is recent, opened by Gérard Parisis in 1994. He is the intelligent chef-cum-owner who abandoned a career in electro-mechanics to set up a restaurant in St-Jean de Côle in the Périgord with his brother. His family had always taken great pleasure in cooking. He then decided to train professionally as a chef. This he did at the reputed Les Abbesses restaurant in Epinal in eastern France. Gérard Parisis recently settled in the Loire with his wife, who works in a laboratory researching on mushroom propagation. The Saumurois just to the west is a massive producer of edible fungi.

Gérard Parisis worked on the building of the restaurant itself. The little dining room contains sturdy furniture and even some benches carved out of the Loire limestone walls, which adds to the cave-like feel. The room with its fireplace is so small that it's the kind of place where it's very difficult not to overhear other people's confessions at the neighbouring table. A little arch leads down to the kitchen. Up above there's a cosy little sitting out area where a small party could possibly take an

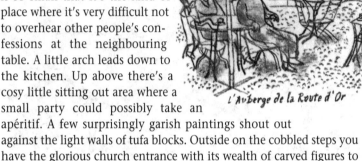

L'Auberge de la Route d'Or

apéritif. A few surprisingly garish paintings shout out against the light walls of tufa blocks. Outside on the cobbled steps you have the glorious church entrance with its wealth of carved figures to look onto.

The food isn't strictly limited to the Loire, although traditional Loire fish and game feature a good deal. Gérard Parisis describes the restaurant's fare as regional cooking *remise à jour*, reviewed for the present times. Presentation counts too in these pleasant surrounds.

There's a simple three-course weekday menu at 85F, but here we concentrate on the 120F and 150F options. On the 120F menu, our friend *sandre* put in its obligatory appearance. We enjoyed the way it was served as a starter here, mixed with salmon in a *terrine marbrée*, although it was stopped from swimming away by the amount of jelly. The *terrine* was peppered with red berries that added a crunchy, hot note. A cooling cucumber sauce accompanied the dish. The other starter when we went in the summer was a fresh melon soup with *copeaux de jambons*, ham shavings, and toasted croûtons, a very refreshing way of serving that old favourite of melon and ham.

Eels popped up on the main course, young eels in a Roquefort sauce. The serpentine form of these fish may make you rather afraid of them, unless you're already a fan of eels, mash and liquor, but *anguilles* are one of the great Loire fish. Here they had been cooked in very tender little pieces and weren't at all hard or difficult to eat as they sometimes can be. They were smothered with the rich Roquefort sauce. Roquefort is by no means a traditional Loire cheese, but it went particularly well with the eels, its touch of blue sweetness setting off the slight bitterness that eels can have. The *confit* of young pork came in a sauce made with very local Saumur-Champigny wine, while the home-made tripe was flavoured with Muscadet, a wine from down the Loire near Nantes.

Venison often appears on the 150F menu. Several large forests are still maintained along the Loire, containing much game. One of them is to be found just to the east of Candes, the Forêt de Chinon, stretching between the Vienne and the Loire. To the north of the Loire here, above the vine territories of Bourgueil, further forests conceal the mighty castles-cum-hunting lodges of the Château de Gizeux and the Château de Champchevrier. The *pavé de biche*, a doe steak, was set off by a bitter-sweet cherry sauce. This might have been preceded by a

flan of asparagus and langoustines with a lemony sauce, an excellent juice to accompany both main ingredients. Or, more outrageously, the young warm artichoke came served with foie gras, another interesting combination of textures and tastes. So many river banks in the region may make you think not just of fish a-jumpin; frogs' legs also made it onto the 150F menu as a starter, prepared in pastry and served with a watercress butter.

For pudding you could settle for a simple sorbet. The glacé pudding in mauve and red tones was more exciting. The main portion of each slice was a *merinque italienne* made with eggs whites cooked to 120 degrees, a coulis of raspberries and cream added. A deep-tinted blackberry-coloured *granité* gave an additional cooling pleasure to the chilled dessert, which had then been covered with fresh raspberries. The pudding's delicious sweet sharpness woke us up for the afternoon.

Anguilles au Roquefort

Serves 4

750g/1 ½ lbs young eels, skinned and gutted
50g unsalted butter
3 large spring onions (with some of their green stalks), thinly sliced
200ml/7fl oz Crémant de Loire or other sparkling white wine
100ml/4fl oz fish stock
200ml/7fl oz crème fraîche
75g/3oz Roquefort (Papillon label preferably)
750g/1 ½ lbs new or tiny potatoes, scrubbed
1kg/2lbs fresh spinach, thoroughly washed
pepper, no salt

Cut off with scissors the bones from the backs and stomachs of the eels. Cut off their heads and tails and throw them away. Cut the prepared pieces into 5cm/2in-thick slices. Melt the butter in a high-sided frying pan. Lightly brown the slices of eel in the butter, then add the spring onions. Deglaze the pan with the Crémant de Loire. Cook until the liquid has reduced by half, then stir in the fish stock. Continue to cook until this has reduced by half before adding the crème fraîche and simmer, stirring from time to time, until the sauce has thickened.

Meanwhile, boil or steam the potatoes until tender. Also, put the spinach, still wet from washing, into a large saucepan with a tight-fitting lid and cook over a medium heat for just a couple of minutes or so. Cut the Roquefort into small pieces and add them to the pan. As soon as the Roquefort has melted, season with a little pepper (no salt is needed) and serve with the potatoes and spinach.

---

touring around

The burial place of the Angevin Plantagenet kings of England; the greatest vestiges of a monastic establishment left standing in France; the first in a special order of monasteries founded from the early 12th century; originally set up as an ascetic community by Robert d'Arbrissel but to become one of the richest royal religious retreats in the realm; under Napoleon demoted to serve as a prison which incarcerated one of the worst of France's literary *enfants terribles*, Jean Genet... Only in 1963 was the **abbey of Fontevraud** (*open June–3rd Sun in Sept, 9–7; rest of year, 9.30–12.30 and 2–6*) acquired by France's state heritage department (to become the largest site of restoration of an historic monument in France) and only then were the prisoners replaced by tourists. Today, the emptiness of most of its great spaces gives little idea of the busy communities which once brought life to it, but the architecture impresses with its grandeur, including the largest cloister in France and the unique 12th-century fishscale-roofed kitchen. Fontevraud's greatest and most surprising claim to fame alongside the Plantagenet royal tombs and the architectural legacy is the fact that, quite exceptionally, especially for the Middle Ages, throughout virtually all the abbey's history women ruled the roost in this, a religious establishment set up for both sexes.

From as early as 1106 the community at Fontevraud was divided into four groups, a separation which then dictated the architecture of the abbey. The principal section, the Grand Moûtier, was the convent for young women of noble birth and widows of good virtue dedicated to a contemplative life. Repentant women and women who had been married several times, as well as lay sisters, were settled in the convent of La Madeleine, devoting their attentions to manual labour. Lepers, meanwhile, were tended by sisters in the Prieuré St-Lazare, set a little distance away from the other buildings. The men were given the monastery of St-Jean-de-l'Habit (short for *habitation*).

Henri Plantagenêt stayed at Fontevraud before he set off for England to be crowned King Henry II in Westminster Abbey in 1154. Two of his children, Joan and John, were educated for several years at the Angevin abbey. And, most famously, Henry II was buried at Fontevraud in 1189. This was not as he had wished, but as his son Richard Cœur de Lion dictated. Such was the displeasure that this difficult son of his had caused Henry through his lifetime that one chronicler claimed that at the funeral, blood began to flow from the dead king's corpse in protest at this final act of insubordination!

Henry's widow Eleanor of Aquitaine chose to live at Fontevraud from 1194 to her death in 1204. She even took the veil just before she died. She it was who deliberately decided to maintain Fontevraud as the royal Plantagenet resting place. Her children, Richard Cœur de Lion and Joan, died in 1199 and she ordered a necropolis for them. She in turn was buried here. The tombs lie like matchsticks in the vast and bare Romanesque abbey church.

The village of **Candes-St-Martin** is particularly lovely viewed from the north, across the Loire or the Vienne, as it stands at the point where the last great Touraine tributary pours into the Loire, forming a wide mass of water and announcing the start of the splendid Angevin Loire. The name Candes derives from the Latin for confluence, apparently, and some Gallo-Romans settled here. If you climb the steep path to the top of the village you can get spectacular views of the confluence and of the two rivers forking away from each other into the distance.

St Martin seems to have had a particular affection for this spot. He had a church built here, dedicated to the memory of St Maurice, like him a converted Roman cavalier. Martin, who set up the first monasteries in France, had come to sort out a quarrel between clerks at Candes when he fell ill and died. Many of the most famous early French saints made it here to pay their respects to St Martin, including Ste Geneviève, who helped protect Paris from the Huns, Clotilde, Clovis's wife, who persuaded the Frankish leader to become the first French Christian king, and Ste Radegonde, the put-upon wife of the violent Clotaire. The present dominating solid squat church in the village, dedicated to St Martin of course, was built from 1175. The church was an important place of medieval pilgrimage. Many French kings stopped here. Pilgrims would arrive from the river bank and this may explain why the north porch, held up by an improbably slender column, was given such prominence, facing the river. Human faces and fabulous monsters congregate at the door, the most remarkable lot of the church's many sculptures. The northern side chapel commemorating St Martin probably occupies the site of the original chapel to St Maurice. One 19th-century stained-glass window here depicts St Martin's body being taken up river by boat; the story of his death at Candes in early November 397 and the undignified argument over the possession of his body is brilliantly told by the 6th-century Gregory of Tours in his famed *History of the Franks*.

In the afternoon, head for **Chinon** with its fine medieval houses as close knit as chainmail fighting for space down between the hillside and the Vienne river. The town is dominated by the secure walls of the great ruined castle of the Plantagenet kingdom. The place may be distinctly provincial today, but Chinon retains more than a spark of old courtly glory. It's a magnificent little town, with utterly charming streets and churches behind the busy riverside road and its pollarded trees. For the most dramatic views of the hilltop fortifications, take in the scene from the south bank of the Vienne. Arriving through the Chinonais vineyards from the plateau to the north, by contrast, the sturdy curtain walls remain concealed—you only get a sudden deceptive and comical view of the risibly thin Tour de l'Horloge rising above the edge of the plateau.

This tower, the most interesting part of the visit to the ring of semi-ruined battlements of the Château de Chinon, is now devoted to the memory of the greatest visitor to Chinon, Joan of Arc, who came to find Charles VII who had run off from the English in the Hundred Years War. But the person whose memory most marks the town today, more even than Joan of Arc, was a 16th-century monk, doctor and writer. Rabelais was, after all, much funnier than her.

'*A boire! A boire! A boire!* (A drink! A drink! A drink!)', rang the immortal first screeches of Rabelais' giant-baby Gargantua as he was born through his monster of a mother's left ear. And the baby wanted wine from the start, thirsting for a stiff drink, not your namby-pamby milk. The quest for the '*Dive Bouteille* (the Divine Bottle)' becomes the great objective of the spoof quest in Rabelais's giant cycle. Wine tasters most frequently discover violets and rubies hidden in the wines of Chinon or the Chinonais, grown and produced along the final stretch of the Vienne river as it approaches the Loire. Chinon wines are almost exclusively red, made from Cabernet Franc.

In wine terms a 'château' so often refers simply to an individual wine-producing property with just an ordinary house attached. With several of the best-known Chinon vineyards, however, you get a proper little Loire château thrown in. Among the most spectacular vineyards to visit for a wine-tasting are the Château de la Grille, a little north of Chinon, splendidly visible on the road to Ussé, and the Château de Coulaine, on the way to Beaumont-en-Véron from Chinon.

Cave Meals in the Saumurois

Today we invite you to a candlelit dinner in troglodyte caves. That leaves you with the whole day to play in the Saumurois. This is the lightest, brightest, most cheerful little stretch of the Loire. And yet there's a whole host of fascinating dark sites underground too—the Saumurois is major troglodyte territory.

Saumur is capital of this little region in the very eastern Anjou. There's no prettier town along the Loire, nor any that's much more conservative, bar perhaps Amboise. The place contains an embarrassment of cultural riches. Of course the hilltop castle stands out, not quite as fairytale in looks as its famous portrayal in one of the greatest of manuscripts of the medieval period, the *Très Riches Heures du duc de Berry*. Several museums are locked up inside it. Then there are the grand churches of Saumur. Two great Romanesque ones have been embellished with superb tapestries. Saumur became one of the great French Huguenot or Protestant strongholds in the 16th-century French Wars of Religion. Its academy attracted intellectuals from across Europe. But Catholicism hit back in the 17th century, with propaganda power architecture such as the church of Notre-Dame-des-Ardilliers, a great breast of a Catholic building. The Saumurois is also dolmens territory, their significance rather

Les Caves de Marson

harder to fathom out. One of the largest you'll ever see refuses to budge from its spot in a café on the outskirts of Saumur.

French people imagining present-day Saumur will think of horses and wine. The Ecole Nationale d'Equitation lies in the hills above St-Hilaire-St-Florent to the west. This is the training ground and site for the shows of the Cadre Noir, France's most famous riding school. Don't be surprised if when you go to Saumur there's some equine championship on. The manure from the riding school goes down the hill to the Musée du Champignon to help its staggering cave production of mushrooms. The Cadre Noir developed out of France's military cavalry school. Horses were replaced by tanks in the world wars of this century, and the Saumur outskirts also house an interesting tank museum.

Saumur's wines are well known in Parisian wine bars. A wide range of types of wine is produced in the area, but the best known still wine is the red Saumur-Champigny, made to the east of town. The vines grow on the plateau above the Loire's southern cliffside. Head along this cliffside not just if you want to go and discover some of the wine estates, but also if you want to see some of the most fabulous little troglodyte villages, houses disappearing into the rockface that was quarried for construction stones and then developed into idiosyncratic real estate. Most of the well-known houses producing sparkling Saumur (*mousseux*) lie west of town, in St-Hilaire-St-Florent. They're such a competitive little bunch of producers that each has made its cellar visit interesting. Spirits too are produced in Saumur, Combier a fine orange liqueur rather less well known that its cousin Cointreau, made in Angers to the west.

Head for Doué for the most surprising troglodyte sites of all. You could visit troglodyte farms, the extraordinary troglodyte zoo, a mysteriously carved troglodyte cave... You'll be completely spoilt for choice on this day.

getting there

You're likely to be approaching this restaurant either from the troglodyte territories of Doué or the wine lands around Saumur. Get on to the D960 between the two towns. Closer to Saumur, the village of Rou-Marson lies just north of this road.

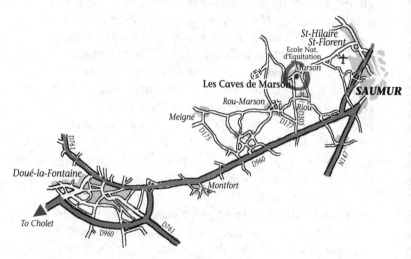

Les Caves de Marson

Les Caves de Marson, 49400 Rou-Marson, ✆ 02 41 50 50 05, ✉ 02 41 50 94 01. You can only eat here if you book in advance. Note that it's only open evenings, except Sun and public holidays: from 1 June to 30 Sept, open Tues–Sat evenings only (from 8pm), Sun lunchtime only. Rest of the year, only open Fri eve, Sat eve, and Sun lunchtime. Annual closure from Christmas to 15 Jan. Menu 115F—which includes a Coteaux du Layon apéritif, a bottle of wine for three and coffee.

The setting of Les Caves de Marson is stunning and amusing at the same time. Once in the pretty village with its sparkling château and church, you enter the property through tufa gateposts, coming into a sweet garden that looks perfectly normal. But the restaurant is beyond the trees and the circle of lawn, behind the several doorways giving directly into the delightful rockface.

On your way in, pause to admire the restaurant façade, the four doorways each in their own style. The most picturesque has a Gothic-style pointed arch, with a little statue of the Virgin in a nook above it. The history of the place isn't entirely clear, but it seems that there was a château on the hillside above it in the early medieval period. These caves may possibly have been quarried to provide first building blocks for the castle and then cellarage space—this is typical of the kind of practical use to which the Loire Valley quarries were frequently put. The old château has disappeared.

Mme. Françoise Joly, who wholly understandably fell in love with the place, did it up and later converted it into a restaurant. She says that it had become an inhabited troglodyte home at one stage, probably a troglodyte farm. She found the oven in place and old animal ties, as well as wine presses in two of the chambers. It is also possible that before the Revolution one chamber served as a secret silo, built to stock grain on which the payment of tax could be avoided. She even speculates that the room with the Gothic entrance may have served as the village chapel in the 14th century. Mme. Joly had passageways dug between the three different troglodyte rooms, which now make the three excellent dining rooms. Cement has had to be used in places to prop up the caves. Mme. Joly comes from the Vendômois on the Loir, which is another troglodyte territory (*see* Chapter 11), so she was familiar with this type of house. When she bought this utterly charming cave dwelling the old oven hadn't been used for decades. She was asked by the *comité des fêtes du village* if she'd open it to the public for a day in May 1978. This went down very well. The daughter of the local mayor knew how to make *fouées* or *fouaces* (explained in the next paragraph) and the oven was revived. Further village celebrations were held here in subsequent years, and it sounds as though the festivities became increasingly Rabelaisian. During one *fête* 600 kilos of flour were used up! Rou-Marson became known for its *fêtes des fouées* and Mme. Joly decided to transform her home into a restaurant.

The main part of the meal are the *fouées*, also called *fouaces*. They are described as *galettes de blé*, normally meaning wheat pancakes; but this type of unleavened bread doughball has the particularity of blowing up when placed in the oven. It's then taken out piping hot, split open, and its hollow interior filled with all sorts of good things.

It's hard to believe that such *fouaces* caused a terrible war in the area to the east known as La Rabelaisie in the Chinonais. The shepherds of Gargantua's country were out at harvest time chasing the starlings from the vines when they saw the *fouaciers* (*fouaces*-makers) of Lerné passing by. The shepherds asked if they could buy some *fouaces*, but their request wasn't simply turned down by the men of Lerné; the latter threw a torrent of abuse on them, their swearing untranslatable in print here. The shepherds responded, with their nut-picking allies nearby, in the only way they saw fit, beating the men of Lerné with their sticks '*comme sus seigle verd* (as on green rye)'. They then helped themselves to some *fouaces*. Thus are wars started. The Picrocholine war that followed is recounted in great detail by Rabelais. The gentle giant's father, King Grandgousier, tries at one point to placate the fanaticism of megalomaniac Pichrochole and his men. He has bakers make for the enemy '*cinq charretées en icelle nuict, et que l'une feust de fouaces faictes à beau beurre, beau moyeux d'eufz, beau saffran et belles espices* (five carts full of *fouaces* that night, one of the cartloads of *fouaces* made with beautiful butter, beautiful egg yolks, beautiful saffran and beautiful spices)'. Unfortunately, even this gift failed to stop the fighting.

At Les Caves de Marson your appetite should be well satisfied by the generous offer. In the fine Rabelaisian tradition of complete gluttony, you can eat *fouées à volonté*. Rabelais champions *volonté*, free will, in the absurdly idealistic imagined Abbaye de Thélème he creates on the Loire's edge at the end of *Gargantua*. Here *à volonté* simply means you can exercise free will as to how many *fouées* you eat. At Les Caves de Marson, they've chosen to create a bit of a women's troglodyte community, Mme. Joly explains. Seven women were cooking and serving here when we went and according to their free will, they were working without men!

The *fouées* may come with a choice of fillings but the menu is totally fixed. It consists of three courses, with a green salad and the bottle of red Saumur between three thrown in. The meal actually starts with a *tarte flambée*. The *fouée* mix is used to make the tart, filled with onions cooked in butter, *lardons* (small pieces of bacon), crème fraîche and sometimes mushrooms. Then the hot *fouées* follow, filled with goat's cheese, *mogettes* (dried white beans, sometimes compared to a Boston bean) *rillettes* (shredded pork meat), or simply with beautiful butter.

The best dining room to eat in is the one with the fireplace, where you could go and look quickly at the *fouées* being made. The big-mouthed oven is heated to a temperature of around 450°F. Piles of wood and the long-armed rakes and oven shovels lie close by, along with trays full of dough. This dough is prepared by M. Sassier, a *boulanger* from Saumur. But even his oven can't match this wood-fed one at Les Caves de Marson. Rabelais writes of *fouaces* being cooked *sous la cendre*, under the ashes. This is no longer the case, but the old name for these *galettes* may come from the Latin for the hearth, *focus*, via the French word *foyer*.

All the cooking is done in the single oven, and although this is two metres in diameter, giving plenty of capacity, expect to wait a little between *fouées*. The food is great fun here, but not particularly sophisticated obviously. That isn't the point. The experience of the place, the atmosphere, is the main thing. The dining rooms are lit by candles, many stuck in crannies in the walls, with the odd intimate corner or else long tables—the place is big enough to accommodate largish groups and can be noisy. Mme. Joly explains with mock seriousness that '*la chaleur de la pierre fait que les gens perdent leur timidité* (the warmth of the stone makes people lose their shyness)'. That's the kind of atmosphere you'd expect in a place with such strong associations with Rabelais.

Pudding is very familiar to Anglo-Saxon visitors—fruit crumble. It may come filled with apples and local strawberries, or peaches with raspberries, or then again apples and walnuts. As you can't make the *fouées* at home unless you have a very special type of oven, and as crumble is rather a hackneyed English dish, with this recipe we propose that you become familiar with *pommes tapées*, a type of dried apple made in other Saumurois troglodyte caves.

Pommes Tapées au Vin Rouge d'Anjou

Pommes tapées are smoked, dried apples that have been hammered into rings, which are only available in the Loire. Bring plenty of them home with you so you can make this recipe! In the recipe it is suggested that the pommes tapées be served as a dessert, but you could also serve them as an accompaniment to poultry or game.

Note that you should prepare the pommes tapées at least two or three days in advance of when you intend to serve them.

Serves 4

8 pommes tapées
1 litre/1 ¾ pints red Anjou wine
50g/2oz sugar
¼ stick cinnamon
5 peppercorns tied in a muslin bag
fresh cream or ice-cream, to serve

Macerate the pommes tapées in the red wine for 12 hours.

Before cooking, add the sugar, cinnamon and peppercorns in a bag. Simmer together gently for around 1 hour. Once the apples are tender, leave them to stand, covered, somewhere cool and dark, for at least 2–3 days. Serve them warmed up, in their juice, with cream or ice-cream.

---

touring around

Given the massive wealth of sites in the Saumurois, one day is very little to devote to the area. In the morning, we suggest that you drive along the Loire bank from Montsoreau to Saumur to appreciate the extraordinary **troglodyte villages** built into the cliffs. Nowhere will you see finer troglodyte dwellings in the riverbanks of the Loire region. Some of the houses have several levels of rock rooms. In certain parts the neatly cut stone blocks of the windows and doors look almost as though they've become overgrown with the wild, natural limestone around, like a kind of enveloping rock ivy.

At **Le Val Hulin**, the main attraction among the troglodyte homes is the **Troglo des Pommes Tapées** (*open July and Aug, 10–12 and*

2.30–6.30, closed Mon; June and Sept, am and pm at weekends, pm only on weekdays, closed Mon; otherwise weekends between Easter and 11 Nov). The First World War tiger of a French prime minister, Georges Clemenceau, ate these carefully squashed apples with his gloves on during his frequent visits to the area; the British Royal Navy was the locals' best customer in times past; American production put an end to the Saumur trade. But in 1890 some 500 tonnes of *pommes tapées* left the local ovens. They're apples that are dried whole and bashed with a little hammer (but you must be careful to avoid bursting them) into compact and tasty little circles. Production here apparently grew to such a large scale with the devastation caused to French vines by the dreaded phylloxera beetle, but Alain Ludin has traced their making back to the late 18th century. Alain shows you how the *pommes tapées* are made in the splendid cave with its *pommes tapées* oven which atmospherically fills the place with smoke at times.

Continue to **Saumur**, where we suggest you go on a walking tour of the town, perhaps wandering round some of its fine churches and streets, or up to the château precinct. The **Château de Saumur** (*open June-Sept, 9–6; rest of the year 9.30–12 and 2–5.30*) still dominates the town's skyline today, but it looks more simply impressive than the ornately roofed version in the duc de Berry's medieval manuscript. From afar it's still a joy to see its silhouette on the horizon, its four main towers stretching like thick upturned pencils into the sky. The octagonal towers and many of the walls date in great part as far back as the 1360s. They were built for Louis, duc d'Anjou, after he had received the county as an *appanage* from his father King Jean le Bon. Having got closer to the château, you realize that it is much sterner than it looks from a distance. This impression is increased by the low outer range of fortifications, with sharp-angled protrusions, added for Duplessis-Mornay, Protestant governor of Saumur, in the 1590s, at a time when the whole realm was on the defensive due to the upheaval of civil war. The château contains a ceramics museum, a museum on the history of the horse and a miniature model figures miseum.

In the afternoon head underground. Back up near the river, just west of St-Hilaire-St-Florent (Saumur's western parish) along the D751 towards Gennes you'll find the **Musée du Champignon** (*open 15 Feb–15 Nov, 10–7*). The horses of the national riding school provide a lot of manure and the quarries dug into the Loire cliff-side lots of dark cool spaces, both essential elements in good mushroom growing. With such advantages, the Saumurois produces the edible fungi on a fabulous scale. It also has this museum on the subject. Button mushrooms are known as *champignons de Paris* in French, but given that some 70 per cent of the national production is grown here, the locals ought to press for a change in its name to the *champignon de Saumur*. On the guided tour of the museum you can learn not just about how the mushrooms are cultivated here, but also about how the limestone was quarried to give these miles upon miles of underground galleries.

The parish of **St-Hilaire-St-Florent** boasts four out of the five big producers of sparkling Saumur. This is the Loire's best-known bubbly, much better recognized than the still relatively obscure Crémant de Loire. Saumur mousseux offers a much cheaper celebratory alternative to Champagne, but tastes much simpler too, with a fruity, fresh openness, rather than any biscuity dryness. Any of the five houses around Saumur makes for an interesting visit, such is the lively competition between them. Bouvet-Ladubay possibly comes out best through sheer number of attractions. Not only does it have its cellars; in the 1990s it has also opened a Centre d'Art Contemporain, with four shows a year, and restored the late 19th-century theatre built for Etienne Bouvet, the place where he and his employees were entertained, with crossed wine glasses standing out among the elaborate period wall decorations..

If you're still hungry for more troglodyte sites, take the road southwestwards from Saumur to **Doué-la-Fontaine**. In this region the troglodyte quarries and homes have been dug down into the ground. This is *troglodytisme de plaine* in contrast to the *troglodytisme de coteau* you will have seen so far. You could visit a troglodyte farm at La Fosse or at Rochemenier, or in Doué itself go to the most fabulous troglodyte zoo or the empty quarried caverns of Les Perrières, which look rather like a wacky Gaudíesque underground cathedral. Roses are Doué's other speciality, grown in vast numbers on its territory. A couple of old-fashioned rose water distilleries are open in town, while the Musée des Commerces Anciens pays homage to the shops of yesteryear.

A Great Riverside Seat in Anjou

La Guinguette à Jojo

Travel writers develop prejudices too, of course, and it's hard to deny that my favourite stretch of the Loire river is the one between Saumur and the outskirts of Angers. For much of this distance you can travel right by the river on either bank. Taking the north side, you go along the top of the great Loire *levée*, the man-made protective wall started by Henri Plantagenêt, alias King Henry II of England. To the north of this defence river wall lies the extraordinarily fertile Authion valley, stealing a portion of the greater valley here—the two combined are often referred to as the Vallée d'Anjou. Vegetables, fruit and roses are grown in vast numbers on the alluvial sands. There are only very few tourist sites to stop at along the north side. The one exception is the Château de Montgeoffroy, set back above the Authion, and a rare specimen among Loire castles, an almost perfectly preserved late 18th-century home.

The south bank is where men settled from very early times. Several dolmens litter the countryside. Gennes also conceals the well-hidden remains of a Gallo-Roman amphitheatre. The legacy of medieval churches and chapels is particularly remarkable, the most extraordinary church of the lot being the vast Romanesque Cunault, its great tomb-like interior held up by richly decorated column capitals.

Just a little to the south of the Loire, you come down into the very pretty valley of the Aubance. Vines grow there, particularly picturesquely around Brissac. This tiny town boasts the tallest château along the Loire. To the south of the Aubance, the Layon valley parallels it, the latter highly regarded for some of its sweet white wines. It's also highly picturesque, with windmills scattered along its heights.

You should notice one striking geological shift as you move west through this area: the change to schist. Suddenly, after so much beautiful tufa for countless miles along the Loire Valley, the limestone hits against a harder, harsher-looking rock. You'll see the difference very very clearly, around St-Sulpice by the Loire, Brissac on the Aubance, and down the Layon.

getting there

This lunchtime isn't so much about food as about location. For once we don't focus on one restaurant, but signal a couple which have the most wonderful Loire-side seats. These two near neighbours are *guinguettes*, basic restaurants on the water's edge where the action is mainly out-of-doors, with live music and dancing often arranged at weekends.

Down from the heights of St-Saturnin-sur-Loire you'll find both: **La Guinguette à Jojo**, Chaloche, ✆ 02 41 54 64 04, quite some distance down from St-Saturnin (*open May–end Aug/early Sept; menus at 125F and 155F*), and **Le Port de Vallée**, ✆ 02 41 57 40, lost by itself between Blaison-Gohier and St-Sulpice, closer to the latter (*closed Dec–March; menus at 85F and 110F*).

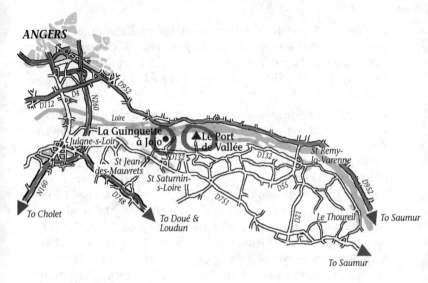

Loire Guinguettes

These are restaurants to be enjoyed on a warm summer's day. Then you can sit outside spending hours gazing dreamily at the Loire waters slipping by. **La Guinguette à Jojo** has the most extraordinary setting. The place itself isn't in the least bit *soigné*, but it's as atmospheric as a slow, romantic French movie. The ride down from St-Saturnin seems almost to take you back in time. When we went it was the kind of hazy summer day where the sky looks as faded as on an old photo.

The restaurant itself is makeshift; you couldn't properly talk of any buildings. But in front of its shacks, what seem like hundreds of plastic chairs and tables are laid out on brown gravel. And splendidly languid drooping branches reach down to give you shade. The occasional geranium pot has been attached to a tree trunk here and there, and little patches of ground have been fenced off in an attempt to allow roses to grow. Strings of coloured light bulbs stretch over to the covered areas. The decoration there is comically incongruous, photos of mountains and a tropical scene blown up to preposterous proportions.

The lunchtime we were at Jojo's (short for Jocelyne Barrage, who has recently opened another rather smarter restaurant nearby, L'Eden sur l'Aubance at St-Melaine-sur-Aubance) it was sublimely calm. Just the sound of rustling leaves and birds singing, and the chatter from the kitchen, the odd burst of laughter ringing out from there. Yet it was still easy to picture the place at nightfall packed full of people and noise, dancers and overexcitement.

Cormorants were fishing. A rowing four passed by, the cox standing up to shout at the team. A string of canoes came down from the nearby base at Port-St-Maur. Bright green and red buoys mark the navigable channel. The church of La Daguenière stands out firmly on the other bank, its white tower topped by a typical black slate tip. There's a landing place down to the right, with a few Loire *barques* tied up there. You pay for the atmosphere rather than the food at La Guinguette à Jojo. The food isn't particularly good value. Nor did it taste particularly marvellous the day we went—Jocelyne had no doubt been distracted elsewhere. Opt for one of the classic Loire-side dishes. We'd recommend staying with the simple 125F menu. This started with a *salade campagnarde*, a salad interspersed with *lardons* and gizzards. This was followed by a *friture d'anguilles* with *frites*. Eels and chips. This is the classic Loire *guinguette* dish. The eels are plunged in boiling oil for five minutes and cooked without being browned. They're taken out and left to cool. Then a pan is heated, salt thrown in, and the eels placed in the pan until they turn golden. A garlic butter is then added at the last minute. Afraid to say, miles better than your average British eels, mash and bright green liquor. The meal ended either with cheese or a slice of tart. Alternatively, you might like to choose *à la carte*. You could start with an *assiette fumée*, which might include smoked eel, smoked salmon, smoked coley and smoked halibut. As a main course you might then go for *moules à la crème*. Or frogs' legs *à la crème*. There must be plenty jumping around these parts.

Le Port de Vallée, close by, doesn't have as wonderful a location as La Guinguette à Jojo. But it still has plenty of character and the cooking when we went was much better. The restaurant is in an isolated, basic home perched above an old quay, on a *levée*. It isn't shaded by trees, but open to wide skies. Accordion music was playing over the stereo when we arrived. We sat out on the terrace, imagining a *bal musette* here on a weekend evening, couples waltzing to such typical French sounds. The dining room inside is a basic rectangle of a room, with large squares of window giving on to the river. Coloured paper decorations were strung across the ceiling, film postcards simply framed on the walls. A bar gives life to one corner.

A collection of various coloured *barques*, green, red and blue, lay down below, across the poor, rough riverbank. A few picnickers had set up nearby. A sandbank stretched out in the river. We were close to the île Blaison. On the far bank, we could make out another set of large quays below the northern *levée*.

You can get a very reasonable three-course menu here for 85F. We tried the 100F menu, preceded by dangerously seasoned pickles with our apéritif. The *rillettes d'anguilles et de brochet, coulis aux tomates* were extremely tasty, the eel imparting its subtle flavour and dense, almost meaty texture to the mix. The *terrine de volaille* was prepared with sweetening figs. The *terrine de chèvre frais aux poivrons* proved the most refreshing and colourful entrée—different peppers had been mixed in with soft goat's cheese, giving a very good contrast in textures, the lot bound together with jelly.

Nettle shoots added an amusing touch to the *brochet au beurre blanc* for main course. The *beurre blanc* was well executed here, nice and buttery indeed. Two purées, one deeply orange of carrots and one, slightly sweet, of parsnips, helped us to lap up the sauce. The grilled salmon was set off by a raspberry butter sauce. There was sea fish too, John Dory served in sorrel sauce, another traditional accompaniment to fish along the Loire. The *entrecôte* came in an Anjou Gamay wine sauce, while the *filet mignon de porc* was quite tender and enhanced by a *crème moutardée* that went down well. All the wines are local, with many half-bottles of various Anjou wines to choose from. You could try a classic French pudding, a crème brûlée, a fruit charlotte, a fruit tart or a chocolate mousse. The *bavarois chocolat crème menthe* was lightly chocolatey, actually quite refreshing in taste, served with a good liquid *crème anglaise*. The *île flottante* seemed the most appropriate dish being so close to Loire islands, even if it is really a pudding for the seriously sweet-toothed, and a particular delight for children.

The atmosphere changes at these *guinguettes* in the evening. Try going on Friday or Saturday night to see their wilder side. !

Sandre au Beurre Blanc

Serves 4

For the court-bouillon:

2 onions, chopped
2 carrots, chopped
few sprigs fresh thyme
3 bay leaves
small handful peppercorns
1 tablespoon vinegar
2 tablespoons dry white wine
½ teaspoon salt

4 pikeperch or mackerel fillets, each about 200g/7oz
100g/4oz shallots, chopped
100ml/4fl oz dry white wine
2 tablespoons white wine vinegar
200g/7oz butter, diced

Make a court-bouillon in advance by filling a large saucepan with water, adding the onions, carrots, thyme, bay leaves, peppercorns, vinegar, wine and salt and simmering for 30 minutes. Strain and set aside.

To make the beurre blanc, soften the shallots in the white wine and vinegar and cook until only 2 tablespoons of liquid remain. Then, over a gentle heat, whisk in the butter, adding a small handful of the dice at a time, until the sauce is creamy and well mixed, then season to taste.

Meanwhile, simmer the fish in the court-bouillon for about 5–7 minutes, or until the flesh is opaque.

When the fish and sauce are ready, place the fish on warmed serving plates and spoon the beurre blanc over them.

touring around

In the morning, head for the Château de Brissac. If you're going southwest from Gennes, try passing by the thoroughly delightful little churches of St-Pierre-en-Vaux and St-Georges-des-Sept-Voies. As that last name indicates, you'll need a detailed map to find your way round the numerous little roads around here. The **Château de Brissac** (*open July–mid-Sept, 10–5.45; April–June and 16 Sept–All Saints', 10–12 and 2.15–5.15, but closed Tues*), seen from the front, looks like a classical body trying to squeeze out of a medieval one. It has nearly but not quite succeeded. The clash of styles certainly gives it a dynamic feel. Brissac advertizes itself as the tallest of the Loire châteaux, reaching seven storeys in one part. It is enormous, an unashamedly swaggering eccentric of a castle.

The original Gothic château was built for Pierre de Brézé, a courtier who served both Charles VII and, albeit very briefly, Louis XI. He died in 1465, fighting to quash the rebellion against Louis. The Gothic pile was sold to René de Cossé, a powerful minister under Charles VIII, in 1502. The same family, with several illustrious members, has kept hold of the castle since then. Charles II de Cossé wanted to mark his elevated rank on his château and he and his master mason, Jacques Corbineau, are responsible, to be blamed or congratulated, according to your taste, on the major transformation of the family home. As Ian Dunlop, author of *Châteaux of the Loire*, noted: 'Corbineau seemed to dislike the naked wall: he left as little of it exposed as possible. The narrow interstices between the windows are so encroached upon by the stone quoins as to produce, over all the façade, the scintillating, many-faceted appearance of a cut-glass decanter'.

The stone boasts of the family achievements inside as well as out. In the entrance hall, very heavily decorated coats of arms imprint the family honours. You then tour some of the splendid rooms. The grand salon sets the tone with its 17th-century grandeur, highly decorated, with an ornate fireplace, coffered ceiling and Venetian glass candelabra. A Gobelin tapestry depicts Don Quixote, but many of the portraits are of hard-headed family members who knew how to hold on to real power. The most extraordinary decoration covers the enormously long *salle des gardes*. You'll be relieved to hear you don't have to visit all 203 rooms the château is said to contain. After the family picture gallery you get a chance for a quick sit-down in the theatre. Yes, without any hint of it from the outside, this château conceals a stage with auditorium for an audience of almost 200. At the end of the tour you'll be taken down to the cellars for a semi-enforced wine tasting—hardly much of an imposition, except if you're on the earliest visit of the day.

From Brissac you could go for a quick meander along the roads either of the **Aubance** or of the **Layon valley**. Both are highly picturesque. Head towards Pimpéan down the Aubance. To see a pretty stretch of the Layon, take the D748 from Brissac via Notre-Dame d'Allençon south. The land around Thouarcé becomes particularly sharply undulating. Above Thouarcé lies one of the Layon's two tiny specialized appellations producing rare sweet white wines, Bonnezeaux.

Get back to the Loire in plenty of time for lunch. After the *guinguette* lunch, go east along the **Loire's south bank**, keeping as close as possible to the river. St-Rémy-la-Varenne and St-Maur-de-Glanfeuil arepretty enough, but the village of Le Thoureil has one of the greatest Loire-side positions of the lot. In summer, when the river dwindles, the children's swings planted in the sand banks make a comic sight—as do the little sailing boats for the local sailing school. Continue east to Cunault via Gennes.

Descending the steps into **Cunault**'s priory church of Notre-Dame, you peer into the vast tomb of a nave. On a sunny day, it's like a brief, darkly blank vision of the underworld, the initial blackness within contrasting with the blinding white and grey stone outside. You enter one of the largest Romanesque

edifices in western France. Once your eyes have adjusted to the dimness inside, the view towards the apse offers a brilliant salvation of a sight. The main church was constructed from the choir to the west end during the 12th century. The increasing richness of the carved capitals going westwards reflects an artistry that was developing in this period. A staggering number of scenes (probably more than 200) decorate the nave capitals. A bishop caught between two open-mouthed scaly dogs, dragon faces with gaping red mouths, men with their legs splayed, vegetation covering their private parts, a choir of monks singing, combat scenes, armoured soldiers in preposterously precarious poses fighting a lance-carrying devil—you can try to decipher these and many more showing the medieval imagination fighting its monsters.

Return to Gennes to cross the river for Les Rosiers. Then adopt the Loire's north bank heading west towards Angers. The expanses of the great French *fleuve* are at their most staggeringly beautiful here. The coastal light can play tricks on the imagination, making you think you're reaching the Loire's journey's end. It's still some way to go.

Go and have a look at St-Mathurin-sur-Loire, but then head back a little east to turn up to the **Château de Montgeoffroy** (*open mid-June–mid-Sept, 9.30–6.30; last week March–14 June and 16 Sept–Oct, 9.30–12 and 2.30–6.30*), just outside Mazé. This is that fine rarity in the Loire valley, an 18th-century château pretty well intact, in fact pretty well pickled in time. It was built for a successful military man, the maréchal de Contades, at a time when France was endlessly at war with Britain. The maréchal's presence still marks the place, the interiors containing much of the original decoration. Such is the pedigree of the château that Queen Elizabeth the Queen Mother came to stay on a visit to Anjou, a sign of how far the *entente cordiale* has improved ties.

To finish the day, you might like to go east to **Beaufort-en-Vallée** to take in the views of the great Vallée d'Anjou at sunset from the town's dramatic heights.

The Maine's Big Mouth

The Maine is the largest river to join the Loire from the north. If the Maine is often described as the shortest river in France, then in winter you might be excused for thinking it might also be the fattest at the point where it joins the Loire. We should immediately explain that the Maine river is different from the *province* of Maine. The river is a shortlived amalgamation of three rivers, the Loir, Sarthe and Mayenne. These three come down from Maine, the province, now split into two administrative *départements*, the Mayenne and Sarthe, sandwiched between the Loire Valley and Normandy.

The great town of Angers, capital of Anjou (or Maine-et-Loire as the region has been renamed since the Revolution), dominates the Maine river. Angers, like Tours, has an extraordinary wealth of sites. With just a half-day there, you should try to visit its elephantine castle to see the tapestry of the Apocalypse. Very close by, the sculpture collection of the works of David d'Angers constitutes an excellent museum, housed in a brilliantly converted church ruin. The cathedral is close by

tenture de l'Apocalypse

too, imposing and massive, and highly important in architectural terms for introducing the Angevin vault.

The restaurant we propose takes you southwest out of Angers to the great mouth of the Maine. Just beyond lie the beautiful walled vineyards of Savennières overlooking the Loire. Abroad, Anjou is almost automatically equated with sweet rosé wines, which is an unfortunate and absurd reduction of the wealth of wines it produces. Savennières makes one of the great dry white wines of western France. Nearby you can visit the mostly schist Château de Serrant, an aristocratic castle still lived in by an aristocratic family and superbly furnished.

Cross the Loire at the island of Béhuard on the south bank of the Loire, at Rochefort among its vines, you can join the scenic high-road westwards along the river, a delightful route nicknamed the Corniche Angevine.

getting there

Bouchemaine, under 10km southwest of Angers, is well signalled from the centre of the city. Or if you're coming along the A11 motorway, take the exit on the west side of Angers. Bouchemaine

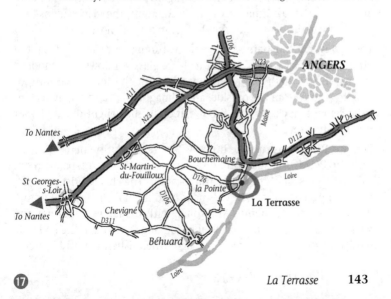

is a favourite spot for Angers city dwellers to get out of town. You need to follow signs for the Pointe de Bouchemaine and A l'Ancre de Marine (the hotel to which La Terrasse is joined) to reach the cobbled square and quays off which the restaurant lies.

La Terrasse

La Terrasse, La Pointe, 49080 Bouchemaine, ✆ 02 41 77 11 96, 🖷 02 41 77 25 71. Menus at 95F (Mon–Fri), 125F, 165F, 215F and 270F.

Cobbled quaysides in towns and villages along the Loire and its tributaries bear testimony to the great river trading activity that once so marked the region. Now many of these riverside ports are charming, quiet backwaters, with their old villages tucked in behind them. The Pointe de Bouchemaine is a beautiful example of one of these old river posts. As its name makes more than clear, it's at the mouth of the Maine. Before entering the restaurant, go down to take a look at the riverbank. You can still see the big old *anneaux d'attaches*, the rings to tie boats to. The flood marker on the quayside gives a good indication that the river isn't always as diminished and seemingly docile as you may see it in summer, with its *épis*, the stabilizing little stone walls running down into the water. The river takes on Amazonian proportions in winter here. Little Loire fishing boats were out in the middle of the river the last time we went. To the right, the view widens into the distance, the gentle Angevin hills rising through the haze.

You can watch the Maine's movements throughout the year from the dining room of La Terrasse with its large glass windows. The modern extension in which the restaurant lies isn't the most charming of buildings seen from the outside, an unimaginative, rather ugly rectangular cement block. Within, though, it offers the delightful flat view of the river horizon.

Bernard Proust has run the hotel A l'Ancre de Marine here since the early 1970s. M. Proust added on La Terrasse in 1990 as a separate room to make the most of the wonderful location. The chef, Christian Fosse, has been here 16 years. The cuisine is traditional French, with lots and lots of fish on the menus. M. Proust, with his languid manner and wicked sense of humour, may well be looking after you at the table. He recalls the days, twenty or so years ago, when fishermen could catch a wide variety of fish in the river. He is the man who claimed to us that it was the Germans who introduced the *sandre* to the Loire—'the only good thing they brought to the place,' he adds.

The choice on the various menus is thankfully not as wide as the river here. The chef seems to have a particular weakness for salmon. M. Proust noted to us that in Louis XIV's day salmon was considered almost as common as muck. Salmon are unlikely to come from the Loire these days. Although some still manage to make it upriver, their numbers were dramatically reduced in the postwar period, no doubt because of pollution, which is only now being fought more effectively. The salmon are gradually returning in greater number.

You can try some of the restaurant's fish dishes on the three-course 95F weekday menu, for example with a starter of a *terrine* of three fish followed by a *mousseline de brochet* and one of the home-made pâtisseries. The 125F menu offers a small choice of classic Loire dishes, salmon *rillettes* or hot goat's cheese *crottin* by way of entrées, escalope of salmon with a sorrel sauce for the main course, a Loire dish you could try making at home. Alternatively, as *plat de résistance* you could choose a *filet mignon de porc au gingembre confit* with its more exotic touch. Cheese or pudding then followed.

We opted for the menu at 160F, starting the meal with a sweet Bonnezeaux apériftif, in special Anjou 1920s style wine glasses. If you enjoy the palate-coating flavours of good sweet whites, you'll be delighted. If sweet wine is anathema, then you could order a bottle of excellent dry Savennières and have a glass to whet your appetite. The choice of Savennières here includes the *crème de la crème* of the *appellation*, regarded by connoisseurs as the Loire's greatest dry white wine, the Coulée de Serrant. Be prepared for the shocking price. There are more reasonably priced Loire wines to try too. In terms of red, look out for the Anjou-Villages.

Oysters from the Vendée not far to the southwest are often available as an hors d'œuvre. A very acceptable alternative would be the leek *terrine* with foie gras, a combination that melts in the mouth. Our choice of main courses was between two classics—*sandre au beurre blanc* and *magret de canard au miel*. The chef is well practised with his *beurre blanc*. There is a culinary argument as to whether this sauce originated in Angers or in Nantes. Duck is often a good bet in the Loire. Travelling along the river between Saumur and Angers you may have spotted a few strange floating shacks on the river, little boats moored in midstream and heavily camouflaged with twigs. These are in fact duck hunters' hides for the privileged few allowed to shoot on the Loire.

By way of puddings, in summer, you might find the soup of fruits extremely refreshing, served with a light *sabayon*. Or a charlotte with Anjou pears and blackcurrants. There might also be a *clafoutis aux cerises* or one of the chef's *bavarois*. The desserts tend to be classic once again, but well executed.

The view over the confluence of the Maine and the Loire distracts the attention from the dining room during the meal. But the interior itself contains some interesting objects including tasteful wooden screens and many 1930s-style touches. There's also a palm tree outside, among some others you can spot at La Pointe, showing what a temperate climate this corner of the Loire benefits from. The locally born 16th-century poet Joachim du Bellay famously wrote of the *douceur angevine*, which sums up so many aspects of this province.

Saumon à l'Oseille

Serves 4

1kg/2lbs 4oz sorrel
75g/3oz butter
500ml/17 fl oz single cream
4 salmon steaks, each about 200g/7oz
salt and pepper

To make the sorrel sauce, soften the sorrel in a pan with 50g/2oz of the butter. Add the cream and, over a medium heat, leave it to reduce a little, stirring from time to time. Season to taste with salt and pepper.

While the sauce is simmering, season the salmon steaks. Cook them in a frying pan in the remaining butter over a medium-high heat for 2 minutes on each side.

Spoon a pool of the sorrel sauce on to each plate and set the salmon steak in the middle.

touring around

The rough medieval pentagon of the **Château d'Angers** (*open June–mid-Sept, 9–7; end March–May, 9–12.30 and 2–6.30; rest of year 9.30–12.30 and 2–6*) forms the most imposing military fortification in the Loire valley. Seventeen massive schist towers stick out around its edges, aptly compared to elephant's feet by many—only they're very much larger than the real thing between 40 and 60 metres high, planted in a wide dry moat. The outer castle was built by order of Blanche de Castille between 1228 and 1238. She was the widow of Louis VIII and served as regent for the young King Louis IX. The walls protect a high platform of land above the Maine. Once across the drawbridge and through the formidably fortified gateway, you enter a château within a château. Lightness prevails within. With its charming gardens and corners protected by the massive ramparts you definitely feel detached from hoi polloi up here. Unfortunately, signs of the cement age have also left their ugly mark in parts. The inner castle now standing only goes back to Louis I d'Anjou, of the 14th century with additions made by Louis II and Good King René. The tour concentrates on the most glorious tapestries and their artistry. The major tapestry work, which draws such flocks of tourists to the Château d'Angers, is the cycle interpreting the biblical *Apocalypse* or *Revelation to John*. It depicts many scenes from this, one of the nuttiest of many nutty biblical texts, with scores of many-headed monsters putting in an appearance. The cycle is housed in a separate under-ground bunker, a 1950s monstrosity. The massive medieval work was commissioned by Louis I d'Anjou. Seventy-six out of the original 84 tapestry scenes remain, miraculously, given tales of terrible neglect. The scale of the artistic enterprise, executed in the 1370s and 1380s, may seem overwhelming to you at first. There are sensible ways of dividing it into more digestible parts. The idea was to show the cycle in six sections. Certain recurring characters begin to emerge quite quickly. The narrator John, for instance, appears in all the scenes, often taking refuge in a kind of sentry box. The detail should absorb you, fantastical and fascinating, often distinctly weird, sometimes extraordinarily beautiful. The text itself and its various interpretations of good fighting evil are deeply troubling. Some recent commentators on the tapestry have detected what they believe to be pointed references to the early part of the Hundred Years War with England. For example, in one or two spots guides can point to places where the evil figures bear the helmets of English soldiers.

After visiting the château, go for a wander around the splendid streets to the north of it. On the Bout-du-Monde promenade you'll find the Maison du Vin, where you can get a good introduction to the wines of Anjou. Or pop into the Logis de l'Estaigner on rue St-Aignan, specializing in excellent pewter ware, still made in Angers. Other highlights in this packed corner of town include the imposing cathedral, which introduced the graceful Angevin arch to architecture, and the Maison d'Adam, one of the most gloriously carved-beam houses in France, at the back of the cathedral. From the Maison d'Adam, the rue Toussaint leads back to the castle, past the **Musée David d'Angers** (*open 12 June–17 Sept, every day, 9–6.30; rest of the year, 10–12 and 2–6, but closed Tues*), the plastercasts and medallions by the locally born sculptor given an excellent idea of 19th-century French civic pride and the major public figures of the first half of that century.

Leaving Bouchemaine after lunch, you come into the prosperous and picturesque **vineyards of Savennières** which produce that extremely exclusive and elusive dry white wine. It's relatively hard to see the vines, as many of the vineyards are enclosed behind high stone walls. You could try penetrating one of these for an estate visit.

Go down to the bridges across the Loire. You can easily miss the lovely **Ile Béhuard**. Much of the island is regularly submerged in winter and the houses have frequently found themselves *les pieds dans l'eau*, with their feet in the water. You can understand why the adorable little church was perched on top of a rock below which the village clusters. The story goes that King Louis XI ordered the church to be built after he escaped drowning around here.

The **Château de Serrant** (*visits on the hour: open July and Aug, 10–11.30 and 2–5.30; April–June and Sept and Oct, same times, but closed Tues*) lies just northwest of here. Mixing the rough with the smooth once again, the outer sides of the three wings of the château are built principally of irregular pieces of schist, but then the windows are solidly surrounded by finely cut tufa. Within the courtyard, the walls have turned to pure tufa, blinding in the summer sunshine. Though begun in the middle of the 16th century, building work on the Château de Serrant extended over more than 150 years, but the harmony of design was maintained.

Before you enter the living quarters you're taken to see the chapel . It serves as a splendid black and white mausoleum for the marquis de Vaubrun. He died a supposedly glorious death at the battle of Altenheim in 1675. He it is depicted in the laudatory sculpture by Antoine Coysevox, winged Victory floating down from on high to crown him. He reclines periwigged, togaed, semi-naked, seemingly unaware of the laurel wreath Victory has destined for his head. This chapel is a place charged with family emotion. An exiled Irish family, the Walshes, became the proprietors of Serrant and faithful supporters of the Stuarts and Bonnie Prince Charlie. The imposing stone arch gateway, the principal entrance to the château courtyard, carries the Walsh family coat of arms, with three swans, one pierced by an arrow. These arms recall a pretty story of an ancestor wounded in battle and left in the water to die, but rescued by two of the beautiful birds.

Entering the château by the stairway, the barrenness of the outer courtyard gives way to some extremely sumptuous rooms full of the extravagance of Ancien Régime noble living. The staircase itself is worthy of admiration, with its sophisticated coffering containing stylized flowers. From the start, fine tapestries, paintings and a diversity of objets d'art adorn the rooms. The number of *écritoires*, or writing cases, and writing tables might make you imagine that these aristocrats had nothing better to do than to idle away their days writing letters to each other. The Loire formerly flowed much closer to this great house, but the château's outer walls are still luminously lit by splashes of sunlight from the moat on sunny days.

From Châteaux to Slate Mines

La Table du Meunier

Anjou produces much of the dark slate that roofs not just Loire châteaux but also so many ordinary homes along the Loire. In the sunshine, the slate shimmers with colour, in particular with silver and blue flashes. Like the extraction of tufa limestone, slate mining was no piece of cake in centuries gone by. Some of it took place around Angers, much of it in northwestern Anjou, on the border with the province of Maine, towards which we head for the day.

On the way up from Angers there are a couple more imposing châteaux, both prefixed by the word Plessis. Le Plessis-Bourré is much the more picturesque of the two, still in light limestone, properly moated, immaculate-looking, but concealing the most improper painted ceiling along the Loire. Le Plessis-Macé protects itself behind more forbidding schist defences.

The village of Chenillé-Changé where our restaurant is to be found lies by the banks of the Mayenne. You could go boating from the delightful little port. Or you could spend an afternoon down a slate mine. It's an excellent tour for reminding you of the blood, sweat and tears of working people on which so much of the great Loire architecture was built.

getting there

From Angers, take the N162 in the direction of Laval. At Le Lion d'Angers, switch very briefly to the D770 in the direction of Champigné to cross the Mayenne. As soon as you're over the other side, turn north up the D287 that roughly parallels the water until you arrive at Chenillé-Changé. The restaurant stands on the south side of the village, opposite a neo-Renaissance Loire château, but draws attention to itself by its lovely schist walls and strange wooden sculptures.

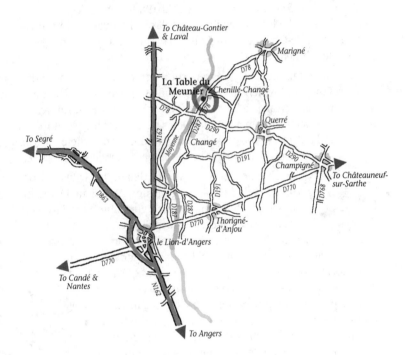

La Table du Meunier

La Table du Meunier, Chenillé-Changé, 49220 Le Lion-d'Angers, © 02 41 95 10 98/83, @ 02 41 95 10 52. Open every day in July and Aug; otherwise closed Mon pm, Tues and Wed; closed for annual hols Feb and early March. Menus at 99F, 129F, 149F, 159F, 175F, 179F and 239F.

This beautiful schist house has irregular windows and a delightful slate roof. The millefeuille layers of stone have tinges of orange and brown as well as black. The entrance to the restaurant lies opposite the grounds leading to that neo-Renaissance château in a style that became popular among the wealthy in 19th-century Anjou. This one was planned by one of the best-known names in neo-château architecture, René Hodé. Back with La Table du Meunier, the wood-carved statues you'll scarcely be able to miss are by an American artist, Fred Close, who came boating here in the mid-1980s. A *meunier* is a miller in French, and the local one with his mill on the riverside in the village of Chenillé-Changé would only have had a very short way to come to lunch here.

The dining rooms are cosy. We were shown into a beamed one with a fireplace on top of which stood little models of windmills. The rustic straw-seat chairs creaked a bit as we sat down. The rustic furniture was placed on superb iron-ore-coloured tiles. There are further such rooms and outside, at the back, is a courtyard-like area where you can also eat in summer. The restaurant is actually quite large.

The chef here is Noël Godin. He and his wife are from the Pays de la Loire region and Monsieur learnt his cooking with his mother and grand-mother. This place was a *crêperie* before the local Bouin family, the present owners, bought it in 1987 and transformed it into a more elaborate restaurant. Noël Godin's cooking is traditional, using local produce such as goat's cheese, duck, Anjou wine and other ingredients for typical Loire sauces. Apples feature in various telling guises, for example in cider and Calvados, signalling an important geographical frontier—we have reached that crucial dividing line between northern, apple and cider country France, and more southerly grape and wine territory Gaul.

There are all sorts of menus to choose from. The 99F menu features familiar dishes: a duck magret salad and home-smoked salmon for entrées, although there was also a choice of a stew of little scallops and cockles in dry cider, which made a change; for main course, fish in sorrel sauce, pork in sweet wine or a steak with shallots. (The Maine-Anjou cow, red and white and reared to give meat, was first bred in the region.) Cheese or pudding follow— look out for Angevin pears.

The *menu du terroir* at 159F offers four courses, but is good value, as an apéritif and a half-bottle of either Anjou red, Anjou white or mineral water is thrown in. It's good to be forced into trying a Coteaux de l'Aubance before the meal, as you might not bother otherwise. We were given a *demi-sec*, not as sweet as some ordinary Layon wines we've tried.

What may have become a Loire favourite of yours by now, eel *terrine*, comes in a light sauce flavoured with Calvados—one of several little hints of northern France on the menu. Eel can be fished in the Mayenne in season. The beige pâté is flavoursome, served with a light mayonnaise, cream and chives adding their tastes besides the Calvados. The cream of onion soup is given extra substance by *rillauds*, Anjou's equivalent to Touraine *rillons*, pieces of pork cooked in pork fat.

For our main course the choice was between *beurre blanc* and *beurre blanc*, either with *sandre* or with farmhouse duck magret with apples (there you go, northern apples again). To be honest there was a third option, *sandre châtelaine*, an old Angevin recipe which contains shallots, like a *beurre blanc*, but does without the vinegar incorporated into the latter. At other times there may be *filet mignon de porc aux Coteaux de l'Aubance*, the wine we tasted as an apéritif put to culinary use.

The *salade de chèvre chaud* is local, from Montreuil-sur-Maine and Angevin pears are often on the menu for pudding of course. Pears are probably the most typical fruit of Anjou. The splendid fat, juicy Comice pear was created here. You may also come across the Passe Crassane, an excellent winter pear. Rarer still, are two very old varieties, the Louis Bonne d'Avranches and the Duc de Bordeaux (the latter a small green pear). For the pudding of *poire belle angevine*, however, the Conference pear is used, cooked in Aubance wine as opposed to being poached in red wine as you may be more familiar with. It can be served with a *crème anglaise*, a liquid French custard. Another fruit that may be on the menu is the *reine claude*, the greengage plum, named after the wife of King François I and seemingly introduced to France and the Loire (when the king and queen lived at Blois) in the time of the French Renaissance. It's used in the traditional *pâté aux prunes*, a sweet tart with a crusty top.

Filet Mignon de Porc à l'Aubance

Serves 4

4 pork fillets, each about 150g/5oz
100g/4oz butter
50g/2oz carrot, sliced
50g/2oz onions, sliced
500ml/17fl oz crème fraîche
500ml/17fl oz Côteau de l'Aubance or other white wine
50g/2oz plain flour
salt and pepper

Preheat the oven to 180°C/350°F (gas mark 4). Trim the pork and keep the trimmings. Place the fillets on a greased baking sheet, season with salt and pepper and roast in the preheated oven for about 20 minutes.

Meanwhile, put the pork trimmings, carrots and onions into a frying pan. Cook over a high heat, stirring until they brown. Deglaze the pan with the wine and cook until the liquid has reduced by about a third. Melt the butter and mix in the flour to make a roux. Stir this into the sauce until well mixed and thickened. Add the crème fraîche. Season to taste with salt and pepper. Whisk in a knob of butter just before serving with the pork fillets.

---

touring around

Invitingly formal, white and moated on the outside, with the shock of the weirdest ceiling along the Loire inside, you'll find the **Château du Plessis-Bourré** (*open July and Aug, every day, 10–5.45; March–June and Sept–Oct, 10–12 and 2–5.45, but closed all Wed and Thurs am; Feb and Nov afternoons only, 2–5.45, but closed Wed*) between the Mayenne and the Sarthe rivers, near Ecuillé. (From Angers, leave the N162 to Laval at Montreuil-Juigné for the D768. Turn east onto the D74 to reach the château.) As you approach this château along a long alley of tall, noble trees, you can imagine King Charles VIII's representatives arriving on horseback at this relatively remote but extremely refined country house to greet the king of Hungary's emissaries in 1487; it would have provided a suitably ambassadorial setting. A cavalcade consisting of some 200 horses came, the Hungarians bringing their own musicians to provide entertainment. Le Plessis-Bourré was then the swanky modern home recently built for Jean Bourré, renowned faithful minister to Louis XI, 'most trusted master of an untrusting king', as the writer Ian Dunlop summarized him neatly. Although set in flat, slightly uninspiring land, Le Plessis-Bourré does make for the prettiest of moated pictures. While defence was certainly not ignored, nor were the possibilities for gracious living. The walls were pierced with generous mullion windows making the rooms light and airy.

Most of the interior has been substantially altered since Bourré's time, but many of the rooms have a lovely feel to them. But wait until you get upstairs. Then the stunning painted ceiling of the salle des Gardes reveals itself in shades of grey and green. For those among you with delicate sensibilities it might be better not to look up too carefully. The hexagonal panels in the coffered wood include pictures of a woman sewing up a magpie's behind and of Venus peeing, standing up, into a bowl a man holds out below her. One prudish owner's wife covered up the offending ceiling before the Revolution, which may have helped it to survive. Her husband wasn't so lucky. Despite local pressure and protests in his defence, he was executed in Angers in 1794. The meanings of the 24 scenes still remain shrouded in mystery, although they're considered to date back to Bourré's day and to reflect the great period taste for alchemy. Eight of the panels contain verses in old French which seem to reflect popular wisdom. Look out for the pig playing the bagpipes.

Chenillé-Changé itself is a pretty place well geared to tourism. It's the Bouins, the same people who own the restaurant, who run the boats. In fact they seem to own half of the village. They also have a shop selling local produce. The riverside is very quaint indeed: there's a Romanesque church with lovely stonework to form the backdrop; pretty, well-kempt gardens sloping down the bank; and a watermill with a waterwheel on one side, disguised as a crenellated keep that looks as though it's standing guard over the expanse of the Mayenne.

On to black gold in the afternoon. For an interesting tour of a former slate mine, go from Segré along the D775, through the low mine-workers' cottages of Noyant-la-Gravoyère, and then follow the sign to the **Mine Bleue** (*open Easter to All Saints', 10–5*). You have to don a mining hat to go down the shaft. Former miners lead the tour.

The underground caverns don't feel at all claustrophobic, made up of vast atmospheric spaces, with makeshift wooden-plank bridges left high up against the walls in certain parts. The former slate-mining work is explained in a kind of *son-et-lumière* as you trudge from one hall to another. The taped dialogue between workers explains their craft through everyday gossip. Although fairly simple, the French may be hard to follow as the actors speak with heavy accents and their conversation is peppered with specialized phrases and jargon.

The skill and danger of the work started with sounding the face for safe slabs of slate. The best pieces of slate were the slabs known as *perclus*. If a miner acted dangerously by striking at an unsafe *cœur* (heart), he would be punished—*mettre le mineur à la soupe* (to put the miner on soup) meant stopping him from going down the pit. The men worked with *baudets* (donkeys). To cheer themselves after work they even had their own cocktail, the *postillonne*, 80 per cent white wine, 20 per cent Calvados, and a bit of sugar. (You don't get to try this on the tour!) The historical explanations underline the difficult working conditions and the all-too-slow social reforms for the miners. Silicosis, a terrible pulmonary illness caused by breathing in tiny particles of slate, took the life of many a man from the area. The 19th-century writer Zola was the most famous among those who campaigned for better working conditions for the miners.

One cavern is appropriately enough devoted to literature and mythology inspired by the underworld. References are made to Vulcan, to Plato's shadow and to the contemporary French writer Michel Tournier and his acclaimed novel inspired by Robinson Crusoe, *Vendredi ou la vie sauvage*, in which Crusoe undergoes a transforming experience, disappearing for a period into the womb of the earth. The acoustics are so good down here that the giant electronics company Philips apparently considered turning one chamber into a recording studio. A further theme journey through the mines, '*Voyage au Centre de la Terre*', was named after the Jules Verne classic; the author was a native of Nantes close by along the Loire.

Above ground, you can visit the museum and watch a traditional slate-splitter at work outside, the craftsman slowly but satisfyingly slicing off neat tiles from the slabs.

The Loire on the Old
Breton Border

oudon

Ancenis, close to which we eat today, used to be one of the fortified towns guarding the Breton border on the Loire. A bizarre redefining of regions under de Gaulle in the 1960s saw the *département* of Loire Atlantique in which Ancenis lies split off from traditional Brittany.

This day takes you first along the final stretch of the Angevin Loire, starting at Montjean, going through St-Florent-le-Vieil with its splendid high esplanade graced by an abbey church containing one of the finest pieces of French sculpture from the 19th century, a moving tribute to one of the few noble moments in the bloody anti-Revolutionary war, the Guerre de Vendée, that deeply affected this region in the 1790s.

Continue along the winding south bank road to Champtoceaux, and cross the Loire to Oudon for lunch. Around Oudon, red-tiled roofs suddenly start to appear as well as slate ones, another subtle sign of regional change. After lunch, slip back onto the south bank of the Loire and descend into the *département* of the Loire Atlantique from the heights of La Varenne, the most westerly village in Anjou. The D751 continues to hug the Loire, passing by the extraordinarily fertile sandy fields of the Loire's plain. You're fast approaching the southern outskirts of Nantes. Rather than heading into the former Breton capital we veer off southwards into the land of the Breton wine, Muscadet.

getting there

Oudon is around 10km west of Ancenis. The Loire river banks are dramatic here, and Oudon stands out clearly because of its soaring château tower. The hotel lies at the bottom of the village, on a corner close to the railway line that separates it from the river. Coming here by the A11 motorway, take the Ancenis exit. Otherwise the busy N23 passes very close by.

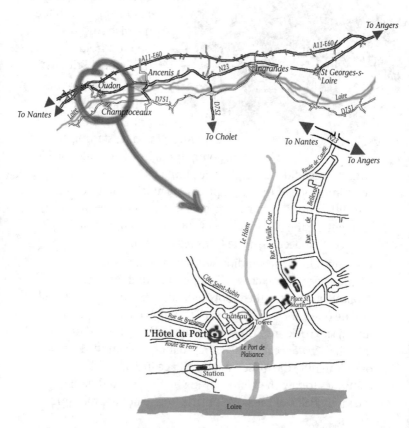

L'Hôtel du Port

L'Hôtel du Port, 10 place du Port, 44521 Oudon, tel 02 40 83 68 58, fax 02 40 83 69 79. Closed Sun pm. Menus at 80F, 120F and 125F.

Curving round the corner of a winding street, the little buildings of L'Hôtel du Port are curiously squashed in against the rock a few hundred metres from Oudon's octagonal tower. Although the Loire is very close by, the hotel just looks on to an unremarkable tarmac car park in front of it. But the building itself has plenty of character and its bar does after all have several Loire views for you to enjoy, painted on its walls! It's worth going for an apéritif in this typical French café. We tried a highly unusual apéritif wine made from a very rare and old grape variety, Malvoisie, a patch of which is still grown in the Ancenis areas producing this honeyish antique of the French wine world.

The *patron* of the Hôtel du Port, Guy-André David, is the man who had the hotel done up after buying it in a state of abandon. The place has apparently always been an inn, with the oldest walls dating back to 1692. It was built partly using the ramparts of the old castle above. A little semi-tropical garden has been squeezed in to one side of the hotel, with palm trees, a greenhouse, a rockery and a parrot or two. M. David looks a stocky French traditionalist. He originates from Nantes. To gain experience as a chef he did his *tour de France*, working in various establishments around the country. He then returned to his native region.

Now Nantes was one of the French towns that grew massively wealthy on the triangular slave trade. Exoticism was imported back and became a feature of the cosmopolitan town. The tradition has continued to some extent, and M. David went to work for a Japanese settled in France, Shigeo Torigaï. The latter's restaurant on the Erdre river in Nantes is considered by many the best restaurant in that city. After you've been presented in this guide with a Loire cuisine mostly associated with deeply rooted traditions, don't be surprised to find some more exotic touches on the menu here, oriental in the main.

Between the bar and the dining rooms lie the kitchens and, outside, a booth from which the hotel sells fresh seafood and ice creams. The two small connecting dining rooms on different levels have been elegantly done up. It turns out that M. David's father was a painter who knew Picasso and Fernand Léger among others. A few of M. David's father's paintings stand up extremely well on their own here. There's also a Léger-like sculpture of the legendary Breton king Gradlon. Prominent Suntory whisky bottles show more signs of Japanese influence.

The choices you're given for the meal are very sensible and good value. We could choose from three formulas. With the first, we were proposed an hors d'œuvre, a main dish and a pudding for a fantastically cheap 80F. With the second we could add a cheese course *and* two glasses of regional wine—a very practical option and still a bargain at 120F. The third formula also offers four courses at 125F. Admittedly for a certain number of the more luxurious dishes there was a healthy supplementary charge added.

M. David makes the most of the fantastic vegetables grown on the Loire's alluvial sands, and of the fresh fish from the coast now relatively close by. The warm leeks in vinaigrette, an excellent way to appreciate the glorious taste of this vegetable, are supplied by market gardeners from the region. Perhaps the best entrée options were those marked *du pêcheur*, 'from the fisherman'. The *croustillant du pêcheur au safran* caught *coquilles St-Jacques* and langoustines in its pastry shell, coloured with a saffron sauce. The *salade du pêcheur* contained fillets of red mullet and skate served hot in a *vinaigrette de pamplemousse*, the reduced grapefruit juice adding a slightly bitter bite. To try M. David's *vrai sushi* the supplement was 25F. He learnt the art from a Japanese master, so he knows what it's about. He uses raw salmon, tuna, and mackerel, soya sauce and sesame oil in the preparation.

On to the fish course, and the *retour de pêche* could just as well be a freshwater fish as a sea fish. So you might be able to taste eel, pike or perch, normally done simply in a *beurre blanc*. *Choucroute* (pickled cabbage) featured a couple of times on our menu, either with coley, or for a supplement of 35F, in a recipe developed by Raymond Pondeville, a *maître cuisinier de France* for whom M. David once worked. M. David is proud of his version of this recipe, packed with sardines, mackerel, tuna and salmon, with some grilled coquilles St-Jacques thrown in. Another option with the seafood were the excellent shrimp ravioli with vegetables, green algae and sea lettuces.

There were standard-style steaks among the meat dishes, but what about trying goose *magret* with a creamy pepper sauce? Or slivers of beef in a ginger sauce? Or *confit de canard* served with shitake mushrooms, meaty and just ever so slightly slippery on the tongue (25F extra)? The Japanese influence crops up again in one of M. David's favourite meat dishes, *volaille japonaise sur salade, vinaigrette de pamplemousse*. The chicken is marinated in soya sauce, the sauce flavoured with Mirin (a very thick, sweet Japanese wine) and ginger.

fromage de chèvre

The cheese brought us back to the Loire, with a lot of goat's cheese. You might also like to risk tasting a tiny portion of *curé nantais*, a potentially lethal little square cheese. If you feel slightly unsettled by the thought of another killer French *fromage*, the puddings are reassuringly familiar—chocolate profiteroles, crème brûlée, orange salad with candied zests... OK, the *fondant au chocolat* did come with a mango coulis. And if you wanted to maintain the exotic thread through your meal, the obvious choice was the *poire aux épices, sorbet poivre*. Yes, that's pepper sorbet with the pears flavoured in a sauce with star anis, coriander, ginger, cinnamon, red wine, and more pepper.

Volaille au Gingembre et Soja sur Salade à la Vinaigrette de Pamplemousse

Note that you need to prepare this dish two days in advance.

(Serves 4)

For the chicken:
100g/4oz fresh root ginger, peeled and grated
200ml/½ pint cane sugar syrup
300ml/½ pint white wine
4 tablespoons gin
400ml/14fl oz soy sauce
300g/11oz diced red peppers and whites of leeks
1 chicken, about 1.5kg/3 ¼lbs, boned and cut into pieces

For the grapefruit salad:

250ml/8fl oz grapefruit juice
200ml/7fl oz oil
100ml/4fl oz raspberry vinegar
pinch fine salt
4 handfuls mixed salad leaves, washed and trimmed

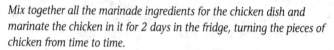

Mix together all the marinade ingredients for the chicken dish and marinate the chicken in it for 2 days in the fridge, turning the pieces of chicken from time to time.

After the 2 days, shortly before you are ready to cook, preheat the oven to 220°C/425°F (gas mark 7). Heat the grapefruit juice until it has reduced by about two-thirds. Leave to cool. Spread the chicken out flat on a baking tray and bake in the preheated oven for about 10 minutes. Look at the tray regularly as the chicken cooks quickly.

Meanwhile, shake the grapefruit juice and the rest of the vinaigrette ingredients together in a clean screw-topped jar and toss the salad leaves in the vinaigrette until they are evenly coated. Serve the chicken pieces on top of the dressed salad.

touring around

Spend the morning patrolling the high road on the south bank of the Loire, looking out on to former Brittany on the other side. From the top of **Montjean**, with its landmark neo-Gothic church on a height, you can walk over to a typical panoramic view from the Corniche Angevine, a slightly scruffy, tufty Loire island far below. The village descends prettily to the very extensive Loire quays, which stretch over some 600 metres and from which a traditional Loire *gabare* sets sail from time to time for tourists in the summer season.

St-Florent-le-Vieil is another cliff-top village with particularly spectacular views next to its church, but the grandiose classical façade should definitely draw you inside. The church contains a moving, even heroic statue of a local hero. As the old bit added on to the town's name implies, little St-Florent has a long and noble history. It was a Celtic site and an early Christian one. The evangelical story has it that the hermit Florent settled here in the 4th century and travelled around to spread the Christian message to the people of Les Mauges, successfully converting them. An abbey venerating his relics was founded on the site by the 7th century, but Breton and then Norman attacks in the mid-9th century caused the monks to flee east, taking the saint's bones with them. They would only return some 100 years later. The new abbey in honour of the saint was established just outside Saumur and this site of St-Florent relegated to a priory, albeit a powerfully independent one. Be that as it may, locals cling to the Dark Ages title and it does look a pretty sumptuous building. In the form you now see it dates from the early 18th century, a fortunate survivor of Republican wrath. The architecture within is a model of Loire brightness, but relatively rare because it's not medieval or Renaissance but soberly classical instead. You can go down via a monumental internal staircase into the blinding neo-Gothic crypt, which has been turned into something of a museum, attractively exhibiting old stones from St-Florent and religious finery, as well as some recuperated relics of the saint himself. But religious memories are, as so often, eclipsed in Les Mauges by memories of the Guerre de Vendée.

With windblown, flowing hair, veins showing out of the veined marble, the beautiful young marquis de Bonchamps props himself up, semi-recumbent, on his tomb. The lower part of his perfect body, paler than a sheet, is draped with a toga. Bonchamps looks like some combination of classical virtue and a Christ of the Resurrection. His head is raised, his right hand stretching up to the sky in a powerful and peace-making gesture. Underneath him, on the slab, his words of restraint, '*Grâce aux prisonniers*'. This statue, with its mixture of political and religious tones, focuses on just about the only noble moment in the Guerre de Vendée. However, its nobility probably sums up the general feelings of many in this region towards the pro-Catholic cause in the anti-Revolutionary uprising. The story is apparently doubly beautiful. The sculptor of this 19th-century work was David d'Angers. His father is supposed to have been among the Republican prisoners saved by Bonchamps's clemency—while Bonchamps (one of the anti-Republican Vendéen leaders) lay dying, he ordered his men to spare the Republican prisoners they held, in spite of the bloody violence the Vendéens had suffered at the hands of the Revolutionary troops.

Windmill in Anjou

If you have time to spare in the morning, go and visit an Angevin windmill, the **Moulin de l'Epinay**, close to La Chapelle-St-Florent (*open July and Aug, 10–12.30 and 2.30–7, but closed Mon am as well as weekend mornings; May, June and Sept, afternoons only, 2.30–6.30, but closed all Mon*). West of St-Florent, red-tiled roofs begin to take over from slate ones, Anjou fast coming to an end. Champtoceaux looks out dramatically over to Oudon and its lone tall castle tower on the north bank, in the Loire Atlantique. The whole medieval town, Châteauceaux as it was known, was laid to waste by Jean V duc de Bretagne in warring over the Breton succession. Some ruins of the fortifications remain. In the Dark Ages, in 768, Pépin le Bref received the ambassadors of the caliph of Baghdad here. Ruminate on that one if you will as you sigh at the views from the promenade du Champalud. From the heights of Champtoceaux it's possible to spy on your lunchtime site.

In the afternoon head back south of the river, towards Muscadet country via La Varenne. The D751 hugs the Loire. You pass by the productive sandy vegetable fields of the pays Nantais and vines crop up here and there. Past Boire Couran, watch out a few kilometres later for the turn south onto the N249. Switch onto the D119 for Haute-Goulaine. The **Château de Goulaine** lies a short distance east of the town. A lovely double line of trees leads up to the château protected behind a plant-covered schist wall. An old square schist tower is reflected in the moat, known as the *tour des archives*. The history of the family of Goulaine here goes back some thousand years. Mathieu de Goulaine, in the 12th century, was chosen by the pope and duke of Brittany of his day to mediate between Louis VII and Henri II Plantagenêt, fighting in the area. Hence the Goulaine shield carries both leopards and fleurs de lys. Another memorable figure in this family was Yolande de Goulaine. Her father had gone on a crusade when the English attacked the château in the Hundred Years War. The troops in the fortress wished to surrender, but Yolande was too proud for that and threatened to kill herself with a dagger rather than yield. This threat was enough to steel the soldiers, who defended the place.

A beautiful new château arose in the last two decades of the 15th century, during the time when Brittany was joined to the French royal realm by Anne de Bretagne's marriage to Charles VIII. It is, surprisingly, in Loire tufa, white and gleaming, shipped down river. So here you have a final flowering of typical Loire architecture before reaching the ocean. The strong vertical lines of the main façade leading to decorated Loire *lucarnes* make for archetypal stuff.

The only break in the great line of family descendants came with the French Revolution. The property was taken over by a Dutch merchant who managed to keep protesters at bay. The Goulaine family regained the family seat and the present marquis, Robert de Goulaine, a crime and wine writer as well as a promoter of his beloved Muscadet, is described as the eleventh in a row. Inside the château you only see a small number of rooms, but they are sumptuously decorated. The tour also includes a visit to the modern butterfly house.

A good place to start a tour of **Muscadet country**, overlooking hectare upon hectare of vines, is the Maison des Vins de Nantes at La Haye-Fouassière (*a short way south of the Château de Goulaine, off the N149; open weekdays 8.30–6.30; weekends 10.30–12.30 and 2.20–6.30*). You can seek advice here on estates to visit as well as admiring the views. One well-known one nearby is the Château de la Galissonnière, the name recalling the French admiral who was governor of Quebec in the 18th century. Another place to learn about Muscadet is at Le Pallet's museum, devoted not just to the wines of the Pays Nantais, but also to the great theologian and persecuted, star-crossed lover Abelard, castrated for his forbidden love for Héloïse.

Finish the day in **Clisson**, where old Brittany combines with old Italy. It makes for a curious and charming sight. The dark romantic feudal ruin of the Château de Clisson contrasts with the campanile of the town's church. Hillside Clisson is all roofed in red, while on the opposite bank of the river La Garenne-Lemot is an Italain villa imported to France, home to temporary exhibitions, and with a park full of follies which you can search for on an evening walk.

Dog Days in Nantes

Nantes is a city that shines. It has an ocean feel although the Atlantic is still some 50 kilometres away and most of the shipping abandoned the port that inspired the Nantes writer Jules Verne some time ago, moving west towards the sea. The city feels delightfully cosmopolitan to the casual visitor. However, a huge historical shadow casts its darkness over all this brightness—the vast 18th century wealth of Nantes was built on the slave trade. The legacy is a mass of rich merchants' town houses, typically decorated with their *mascarons*, grotesque stylized masks.

Somewhat ironically in view of this slave past, Nantes was the place where an extraordinarily important act of tolerance, the Edict of Nantes, was signed towards the end of the terrible French Wars of Religion and the 16th century by King Henri IV, allowing Protestants throughout France the freedom to worship after they had suffered so much persecution. Before those times (and apparently the slave trade went back as far as the 16th century) Nantes was the capital of Brittany for a long line of independent dukes. The last one began the building of the massive château, once on the bank of an arm of the Loire. Other great landmarks in town include the cathedral and the Tour de Bretagne, a modern skyscraper from which you can get a good bird's eye view of the *pays nantais*.

Nantes is apparently where the inland Loire river turns into a maritime one. The so-called port of Nantes-Saint-Nazaire, still in the top handful of the largest ports in France, stretches its industrial activities along a staggering 60 kilometres of the north bank of the Loire—in Nantes itself you can see a rather astonishing industrial site on the island south of the centre of town, with its hills of scrap metal.

getting there

Our restaurant lies to the west of the broad Cours des 50 Otages which divides the heart of Nantes in two, going roughly from north to south. Take the rue d'Orléans to the place Royale, then the rue Crébillon to the place Graslin, with the theatre on one side. Leave that square by the rue Voltaire and continue past the Musée d'Histoire Naturelle and the Musée Dobrée to the place Eugène Livet. Le Chiwawa occupies the southwest corner of this typically elegant Nantes square.

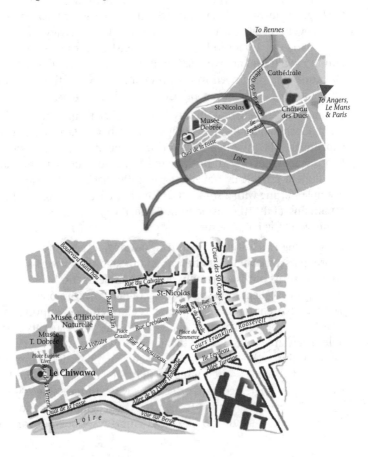

Le Chiwawa

Le Chiwawa, 6 place Eugène Livet, 44100 Nantes, ℗ 02 40 69 01 65.
Closed Sat lunchtime, Sun and Mon lunchtime, as well as on public
holidays. Menus at 115F, 160F and 220F.

In summer, many Nantes restaurants are allowed to build little terraces out into the street, often covering their makeshift raised platforms with astroturf. Le Chiwawa follows the trend, so you can sit out in the square in summer. It's very Nantes. The buildings around are in neat white blocks of stone. The bust in the centre of the square, in front of the large bourgeois-looking house with its garden along the north side, is of Eugène Livet. On the carefully presented and very full menu (which you can ask for in English—the translations can be very entertaining) you'll find an explanation of this man's career in education. Of course you may need to eat inside and there are three intimate dining rooms which seem about the size of ships' cabins.

You may be thinking that this restaurant has been named so peculiarly like a pooch parlour by an overdoting pet owner. In fact Claude Vallée explains that he inherited the name from the Mexican establishment that previously occupied this spot and he found it amusing. M. Vallée has done a fair bit of travelling to exotic places in his career, for example starting with a stint in the Caribbean. He's also worked in the mountains, and at the casino in La Baule, the glamorous seaside resort just beyond the Loire's estuary.

His cooking is traditional, with fish, not dog, a speciality. M. Vallée clearly puts a vast amount of effort and thought into the cuisine; and what he turns out is extremely refined and delicious, his restaurant making an excellent final stop on this culinary voyage along the Loire. The menus are interesting to peruse, each offering a tempting list of possibilities for each course. For a big town, the prices are very reasonable. There are generous little touches too. Even the four-course 115F menu begins with an *amuse bouche*. The dishes have long, romantic, complicated names—they indicate that the cooking is going to be elaborate, the ingredients *recherchés*. The wine list has some 200 references. The excellent map puts the wines in geographical context. M. Vallée bought a lot of the fine 1990 vintage, so look out for those bottles if any are left. The choice of Loire wines is extensive. But if you're concentrating on the fish and seafood, which is top class here, Muscadet is the traditional local drink.

It would be helpful if a dictionary were served with the menus, even with the English translation, which has some delightful little turns of phrase, such as 'pepper of the mill', 'a frying pan of scampi with lemon thyme' or 'Ocean preciousness, scampi whims, cured salmon purse, millefeuille of China violets with edible crab'—the latter all one dish! Such suggestions as ocean lemon squash, *omble chevalier avec pleurotes solette*, weevers, *chaource* and *langre* may intrigue you. You may want to ask a fair few questions before choosing. M. Vallée clearly seeks out the unusual and the exotic. There are of course easily recognisable Loire features too, as well as Breton and Provençal touches.

Among the first, four-course menu starters, the *gratin de lan-goustines* came with *al dente* vegetables in a sea urchin cradle, with a sabayon flavoured with Saumur white wine on top. Simply delicious, a typical example of what the chef can produce—and scarcely the kind of little dish you'll rustle up any evening at home! Seafood features in most of the entrées throughout the various menus. Fresh langoustines, *pétoncles* (queen scallops), *encornets* (squid), *huîtres* (oysters), *bigorneaux* (whelks) and many other shells appear time and again, with the main fish and meat dishes as well. The squid might come in ravioli with snails, accompanied by a winkle stew. On the five-course 220F menu, you may find it hard to believe that things are taken a stage further: entrées included pigeon and duck liver with ginger, served with a dandelion liqueur; the *salade folle* had an extraordinary list of ingredients, *sots-l'y-laisse*, *sandre* cheeks, quail 'haunch', marinated monkfish, little cockles, more duck liver, and pieces of truffle. The pan-fried langoustines in young rabbit juice, puffed wheat served with wild thyme and a *julienne* of fried leeks sounded quite basic by comparison. Some of the ingredients and tastes may be unknown to you, so you should be able to make some culinary discoveries here.

The cheese is chosen with as much care to detail and originality as the other courses. The *chaource* and *langre* are among the unusual selection, these two hard and mature cow's cheeses. Goat's cheese continues into the pudding choices. *Nos trois crèmes brûlées* are made with the stuff, and flavoured with coffee, vanilla and pistachios. Caramel ice cream added more sweetness to that dessert. The *songe autour d'une pomme* is a dish of typical simplicity in this restaurant, given below for you to have a stab at. *Fressinettes*, by the way, haven't anything to do with strawberries, but are a type of banana. Pears feature too of course, with mountain honey and a more serious sorbet flavoured with Poire Williams liqueur. We couldn't possibly leave the Loire Valley without another reverential mention of the *tarte des demoiselles Tatin*. Purists say that it should be served by itself. Here though, you won't be surprised to hear, it's really frilled up, with green apple sorbet, pecan nuts and flambéd with Calvados!

Songe Autour d'une Pomme

An array of delicate apple puddings.

Serves 4

For the Tartes Fines aux Pommes:
225g/8oz puff pastry
8 apples, 4 peeled, cored and chopped, 4 sliced extremely thinly
100ml/4fl oz water
100g/4oz sugar
2 tablespoons brown sugar

For the Balluchons avec Crêpes:
50g/2oz plain flour
pinch salt
1 egg
150ml/¼ pint milk
½ tablespoon butter or oil, plus butter or oil for frying
4 apples, peeled, cored and chopped
4 tablespoons Calvados

For the Gâteaux Grand-mère

4 apples, peeled, cored and chopped
25g/1oz butter
50g/2oz sugar
30g/1¼oz powdered gelatine
4 egg yolks
a little caster sugar, for coating
2 tablespoons brown sugar

For caramel sauce:

100g/4oz sugar
150ml/¼ pint cider

To serve:

4 scoops green apple sorbet

For the **Tartes Fines aux Pommes**, preheat the oven to 220°C/425°F (gas mark 7). Roll the pastry out to about a 5mm/¼in thickness and line 4 greased individual tart tins. Set to one side. Prepare some apple compôte by simmering the apples, water and sugar together until the apples break down. Put the compôte into the pastry cases, then overlap the thin apple slices in a circle on top of each one. Sprinkle the brown sugar evenly over the top of each tart and bake in a preheated oven for about 10–15 minutes. Keep warm.

For the **Balluchons avec Crêpes**, thoroughly mix together the flour, salt, egg, milk and butter or oil and leave to stand for an hour or so. When you are ready, heat a little butter or oil on a frying pan and make 4 crêpes. Stack with a layer of greaseproof paper between each and keep warm. Sauté the apples in the Calvados until golden. Keep warm.

For the **Gâteaux Grand-mère**, preheat the oven to 170°C/325°F (gas mark 3). Then sauté the apples in the butter until they have softened and add the sugar. Remove the pan from the heat and stir in the powdered gelatine. Quickly stir in the egg yolks. Spoon the mixture into 4 individual flan tins that you have greased and coated with caster sugar. Place the little flan tins in a roasting tin and pour in water to come halfway up the sides. Bake in the preheated oven for 35 minutes. Run a knife round the edges of each flan tin and invert sharply on to a heatproof and flameproof *plate. Sprinkle a little brown sugar over each and cook briefly under a very hot grill to caramelise. Keep warm.*

*Next, make a **caramel sauce**. Put the sugar and water into a small pan. Stir over a gentle heat until the sugar has dissolved, then raise the heat and boil the syrup until it becomes a rich brown colour, without stirring (if you stir, the caramel may crystallise).*

Just before serving, divide the apples in Calvados between the crêpes, roll them up and lay, seam-side down, on a serving plate. Place a tarte and a gâteau next to the crêpe on each plate, add a scoop of apple sorbet and encircle them all with a ribbon of caramel sauce.

---

touring around

The **Château de Nantes** is almost as forbidding as Angers's fortifications from the outside, massive dark walls once again enclosing slightly more graceful white wings within. A deep broad moat, where many Nantais now take their dogs for a walk, separates the building from the boulevards around. Originally the Loire lapped at the walls.

The main structure was built for François II, the final duc de Bretagne. He considered the previous 13th-century construction unbefitting to his court and from 1466 had work commence on this mass, both defensive and palatial. Anne de Bretagne, his daughter, added embellisments, as did the French king François I, who came here to declare the union of Brittany to France in 1532, as a plaque commemorates. He had received the Château de Nantes (built on the kind of scale he appreciated) as part of the dowry of his first wife, Claude de France, daughter of Anne de Bretagne and Louis XII. He and many other visitors here would often use the château's river exit to travel by water to other castles along the Loire.

Henri IV received the Huguenot leaders here to work out the Edict of Nantes. Madame de Sévigné, that superlative 17th-century correspondent, stopped here to see her cousin on her extraordinary trip down the Loire by *coche d'eau*. After the end of the Ancien Régime, the château was turned into a barracks, while early on in its new military phase, in 1792, a good number of priests were detained here by Revolutionary authorities before being sent packing to Spain.

On entering the courtyard you don't know exactly where to look. The architecture is something of a mess, to put it mildly, what with the irregular shape of the site and the diversity of buildings from across the centuries calling for your attention or distracting you. This is probably the least harmonious château along the Loire. But the castle contains a clutch of Nantes museums. Temporary exhibitions are held in the Tour du Fer à Cheval. The Bâtiment du Harnachement has also been restored for exhibitions. The Grand Gouvernement contains the Musée des Arts Décoratifs. This includes displays of regional costumes and furniture, ironwork and pottery. Work has been continuing on further transformations, so you may find further surprises when you go.

The **cathedral of St-Pierre**, which you can reach via the grand *cours* just east of the château, stands squatly on a hill a little north of the castle. While the exterior is rather grey, this is in strong contrast to the inside, which is blindingly white, brushed brilliantly clean after a terrible fire in 1972. Only a few patches of burnt marks can be seen on certain pillars holding up the white Gothic arches. The uncluttered monuments tend to be even whiter still. This is the cleanest inside of a cathedral you're likely to see. Work began on it in 1434 under Jean V, duc de Bretagne, and the bishop Jean de Malestroit, on the site of the previous Romanesque building—only the crypt under the present choir survived. The architect was Guillaume de Dommartin-sur-Yèvre. The major artistic interest within lies in the tender tomb of François II, duc de Bretagne, and of his two wives. The work was executed in the early 16th century in the workshop of the brilliant Tours sculptor Michel Colombe.

You should have spotted the **Tour de Bretagne** on the Nantes skyline by now. You may have time to walk to it and take the escalator up before lunch. It's a free ride and from up top you can get your bearings of the city and its two rivers, the Loire and the Erdre. Then head through the shopping, historic and tramway streets of Nantes to the restaurant.

In the afternoon, you might like to go first to the **Musée Dobrée** so close to Le Chiwawa. The golden heart of Brittany lies in this museum. Anne de Bretagne, having given her father's independent province in marriage to two French kings, having seen her daughter Claude married to a third, asked for her heart to be buried at Nantes. The engraved reliquary isn't the only piece of superb craftsmanship on display. The place is full of the finest stonework, woodwork and enamel work in particular, collected by Thomas Dobrée in the 19th century.

After the Musée Dobrée, potter around the beautiful area to the west of the wide cours des 50 Otages. Look out particularly for the elegance of the cours Cambronne and the shopping arcade of the Passage Pomeraye, beloved of Flaubert, situated a little to the east of the place Graslin, the last containing Nantes's main theatre and the culinary cultural site of the Art Nouveau La Cigale restaurant—book well in advance if you want to try to eat there in the evening (✆ 02 40 69 76 41). Head a little south for the café-bustling place du Commerce with the stock exchange turned tourist office and south again over the river-broad (a branch of the Loire once flowed freely here) *cours* to the Ile Feydeau, packed with fine merchants' houses, some of their decadent façades a little dilapidated now.

You really need a car to go west along the north bank of the Loire to the **Musée Naval Maillé Brézé**, a naval ship turned museum run by a team of lively enthusiasts, or up the hill to the Musée Jules Verne, a rather old-fashioned museum in the quarter where the great science fiction writer lived. For a bizarre landscape of iron mountains and semi-abandoned docks, head onto the large island to the south of the centre of Nantes, with its almost unreal atmosphere, recalling in melancholy fashion the great and vibrant river trade that once brought life to the Loire along so much of its length.

A Culinary Glossary

The full French culinary vocabulary is
enormous, and several pocket guides are
available that give extensive lists of the
many terms and phrases. The following should,
though, provide some of the necessary basics.

Useful Phrases

I'd like to book a table (for two/at 12.30pm)	*Je voudrais réserver une table (pour deux personnes/à midi et demie)*
lunch/dinner	*le déjeuner/le dîner*
Is it necessary to book for lunch/dinner today?	*Est-ce qu'il faut réserver pour déjeuner/dîner aujourd'hui?*
Waiter/Waitress! (to attract their attention)	*Monsieur/Madame/Mademoiselle! S'il vous plaît*
The 130F menu, please	*Le menu à centtrente francs, s'il vous plaît*
Which are your specialities?	*Quelles sont les specialités de la maison?*
What is (this dish), exactly?	*Qu'est-ce que c'est exactement, (ce plat)?*
The wine list, please	*La carte des vins, s'il vous plaît*
Another bottle of wine, please	*Une autre bouteille, s'il vous plaît*
water (from the tap, perfectly good in France, and usually given as a matter of course)	*une carafe d'eau*
mineral water/fizzy/still	*eau minérale/gazeuse/plate*
coffee (espresso)	*café*
white coffee	*café au lait /café crème*
That was wonderful	*C'était formidable/délicieux*
We've enjoyed the meal very much, thank you	*Nous avons très bien mangé, merci*
The bill, please	*L'addition, s'il vous plaît*

Poissons et Coquillages (Fish and Shellfish)

anguille	eel	langoustine	Dublin Bay prawn
bar	sea bass	lieu	pollack or ling
barbue	brill	lotte	monkfish
bigorneau	winkle, sea snail	limande	lemon sole
brochet	pike	loup de mer	sea bass
cabillaud	fresh cod	maquereau	mackerel
calamar	squid	merlan	whiting
colin	hake	morue	salt cod
coques	cockles	moules	mussels
coquilles St-Jacques	large scallops	mulet	grey mullet
		palourde	clam
crevette	shrimps or prawns	pétoncle	small scallop
daurade	sea bream	poulpe	octopus
écrevisses	freshwater crayfish	raie	skate
escargots	snails	rascasse	scorpion-fish
flétan	halibut	rouget	red mullet
friture	deep fried fish	St-Pierre	John Dory
fruits de mer	seafood	sandre	zander/pikeperch
hareng	herring	saumon	salmon
homard	lobster	saumonette	dogfish
huîtres	oysters	sole	sole
julienne	ling	thon	tuna
langouste	spiny lobster or crawfish	truite	trout

Viandes, Volaille, Charcuterie
(Meat, Poultry, Charcuterie)

abattis/abats	giblets/offal	bœuf	beef
agneau	lamb	boudin blanc	white pudding
andouille	large sausage made from offal, served cold	boudin noir	black pudding
		caille	quail
		canard, caneton	duck, duckling
andouillette	smaller than an andouille, eaten hot	cervelas	garlic pork sausage
		cervelles	brains
biftek, bifteck	steak	chevreau	kid

chevreuil	roe deer; also venison in general
civet	stew
colvert	mallard
cuisses de grenouilles	frogs' legs
daguet	young venison
dinde, dindon	turkey
faisan	pheasant
foie	liver
foie gras	fattened goose or duck liver
galantine	meat stuffed, rolled, set in its own jelly
géline	large old hen
génisse	heifer
gésier	gizzard
gibier	game
jambon	ham
langue	tongue
lapin	rabbit (young)
lard (lardons)	bacon (diced)
lièvre	hare
marcassin	young wild boar

merguez	spicy red sausage
moëlle	beef marrow
navarin (d'agneau)	lamb stew with spring vegetables
oie	goose
os	bone
perdrix (perdreau)	partridge (young)
petit salé	salt pork
pintade (pintadeau)	guinea fowl (young)
porc	pork
poularde	fattened chicken
poulet	chicken
poussin	spring chicken
queue de bœuf	oxtail
rillettes	potted meats
ris (de veau)	sweetbreads (veal)
rognons	kidneys
sanglier	wild boar
saucisses	sausages
saucisson	French salami
tête (de veau)	head (of veal)
veau	veal

Meat Cuts

aiguillette	long, thin slice
aile	wing
carré (d'agneau)	rack (of lamb)
Châteaubriand	double fillet steak, usually with a béarnaise sauce
contre-filet, faux-filet	sirloin steak
confit	meat cooked and preserved in its own fat
côte, côtelette	chop, cutlet

cuisse	leg or thigh
entrecôte	rib steak
épaule	shoulder
escalope	thin fillet
gigot (d'agneau)	leg (of lamb)
gigue	haunch
jarret	shin or knuckle
magret, maigret (de canard)	breast (of duck)
noisette (d'agneau)	small round cut (of lamb)
onglet	flank of beef

pavé	thick, square fillet	*selle (d'agneau)*	saddle (of lamb)
pieds	trotters	*tournedos*	thick round slices of steak
râble (de lièvre, de lapin)	saddle (of hare, rabbit)	*travers de porc*	pork spareribs
rôti	roast		

Cooking Terms for Steaks and Grills

bleu	very rare	*à point*	medium rare
saignant	rare	*bien cuit*	well done

Légumes, Herbes, Epices (Vegetables, Herbs, Spices)

ail	garlic	*échalote*	shallot
algue	seaweed	*épinards*	spinach
aneth	dill	*fèves*	broad beans
avoine	oats	*flageolets*	small green beans
badiane	star anise	*frites*	chips
baies roses	pink peppercorns	*genièvre*	juniper
betterave	beetroot	*gingembre*	ginger
blette	swiss chard	*girofle*	clove
cannelle	cinnamon	*girolles*	same as *chanterelles*
céleri-rave	celery-celeriac	*haricots (rouge, blanc, vert)*	beans (kidney, white, green)
cèpes	wild, large, brown, fleshy mushrooms	*laitue*	lettuce
champignons	mushrooms	*laurier*	bay leaf
chanterelles (girolles)	wild, yellowish mushrooms	*maïs (épis de)*	sweet corn (on the cob)
chou	cabbage	*menthe*	mint
chou-fleur	cauliflower	*morilles*	morel mushrooms
choux de Bruxelles	Brussels sprouts	*muscade*	nutmeg
		navet	turnip
ciboulette	chives	*oseille*	sorrel
citrouille	pumpkin	*panais*	parsnip
cœur de palmier	palm hearts	*persil*	parsley
concombre	cucumber	*pissenlit*	dandelion
cornichons	gherkins	*pleurotes*	soft-fleshed mushrooms
courge	pumpkin		
cresson	watercress	*poireau*	leek

poivron	bell pepper	*radis*	radish
pomme de terre	potato	*raifort*	horseradish
primeurs	young vegetables	*romarin*	rosemary
		sarriette	savoury (the herb)
printanière	garnish of spring vegetables	*sarrasin*	buckwheat
		seigle	rye

Fruits, Noix, Desserts (Fruits, Nuts, Desserts)

ananas	pineapple	*groseilles*	red currants
bavarois	made with whipped cream, egg custard	*macarons*	macaroons
		madeleine	small sponge cake
brugnon	nectarine	*mandarine*	tangerine
cacahouètes	peanuts	*mangue*	mango
cajou (noix de)	cashew nut	*marrons*	chestnuts
cassis	blackcurrant	*miel*	honey
cerise	cherry	*mirabelles*	small yellow plums
charlotte	layered dessert in a mould	*mûres*	mulberries, blackberries
citron/citron vert	lemon/lime	*myrtilles*	bilberries
clafoutis	fruit flan	*noisette*	hazelnut
coing	quince	*noix*	walnut
corbeille de fruits	basket of fruits	*œufs à la neige*	light meringue in a vanilla custard
coupe	ice-cream cup		
crème anglaise	very light custard	*pamplemousse*	grapefruit
crème Chantilly	sweet whipped cream	*parfait*	Chilled mousse
crème fleurette	double cream	*pastèque*	watermelon
crème fraîche	sour cream	*pêche*	peach
crème pâtissière	custard filling	*pignons*	pine nuts
dattes	dates	*pistache*	pistachio
figues	figs	*poire*	pear
figue de Barbarie	prickly pear	*pomme*	apple
fraises (des bois)	strawberries (wild)	*prune*	plum
framboises	raspberries	*pruneau*	prune
fruit de la passion	passion fruit	*reine Claude*	greengage
génoise	sponge cake	*raisin*	grapes
glace	ice cream	*raisins secs*	raisins
grenade	pomegranate	*sablé*	shortbread biscuit

savarin	ring-shaped cake, in rum- or kirsch-flavoured syrup	tarte Tatin	caramelised apple pie, upside-down
		truffes	chocolate truffles

General Terminology

aigre-doux	sweet and sour	chausson	pastry turnover
allumettes	strips of puff pastry or potatoes	confiture	jam
		coulis	thick sauce, purée
amuse-gueules	appetisers	court-bouillon	stock
(à l') anglaise	plain boiled	couteau	knife
assiette de...	plate or platter of...	(en) croûte	in a pastry crust
		cru	raw
barquette	small pastry boat	crudités	raw vegetables
béarnaise	classic sauce of egg yolks, white wine shallots, butter, tarragon	cuillère	spoon
		cuit	cooked
		demi-glace	basic brown sauce, reduced meat stock
béchamel	white sauce of butter, flour, milk	diable	peppery sauce: mustard, vinegar, shallots
beignets	fritters	Duxelles	mushrooms and shallots sautéd in butter and cream
Bercy	similar to a beurre blanc, but thicker		
beurre	butter	émincé	thinly sliced
beurre blanc	reduced sauce of butter, white wine, vinegar, shallots	épices	spices
		farci	stuffed
		(au) feu de bois	cooked over a wood fire
bisque	thick soup, usually of seafood	feuilleté	flaky pastry leaves
blanquette	thick creamy stew	forestière	with mushrooms bacon and potatoes
bouchée	tiny mouthful, or vol-au-vent		
		(au) four	oven-baked
bouillon	stock or broth	fourré	filled or stuffed, usually sweets
(à la) broche	spit-roasted		
brouillé	scrambled	frappé	with crushed ice
brûlé	caramelised ('burnt')	fricassé	braised in sauce of white wine, butter, and cream
chasseur	white wine sauce with mushrooms, shallots		
chaud	hot	frit	fried

froid	cold	*paupiettes*	thin slices of fish or meat filled, rolled, wrapped to cook
fromage	cheese		
fumé	smoked		
galette	buckwheat pancake	*paysan, paysanne*	country-style; with bacon, potato, carrot, onion, turnip
garni	garnished; served with vegetables		
		poêlé	pan-fried
gelée	aspic	*poivrade*	peppery sauce: a demi-glace, wine, vinegar, vegetables
glacé	iced		
grillade	mixed grill		
hachis	mince or minced	*poivre*	pepper
hollandaise	sauce of egg yolks, butter, lemon juice	*potage*	thick soup
		quenelles	dumplings made with fish or meat
huile (d'olive)	oil (olive)		
jardinière	with diced garden vegetables	*râpé*	grated, shredded
		rémoulade	mayonnaise with capers, mustard, gherkins, herbs; also shredded celery
marmite	small casserole		
matelote	fish stew		
médaillon	round piece		
meunière	fish: floured, fried in butter, with lemon and parsley	*roulade*	rolled meat or fish, often stuffed
		salé	salted, spicy
mijoté	simmered	*sauvage*	wild
Mornay	cheesy béchamel	*sel*	salt
mousseline	hollandaise sauce with egg whites and whipped cream	*Soubise*	white onion sauce
		sucre/sucré	sugar/sugared
		suprême	boned breast of poultry; fish fillet; a creamy sauce
(à la) nage	poached in an aromatic broth (fish)		
nature, au naturel	simple, plain	*tiède*	lukewarm
oeuf	egg	*tilleul*	lime (-blossom)
pain	bread	*timbale*	small pie cooked in dome-shaped mould
panaché	mixed, a mixture		
pané	breaded	*tranche*	slice
(en) papillote	baked in buttered paper or foil	*(à la) vapeur*	steamed
		velouté	white sauce flavoured with stock
Parmentier	with potatoes		
pâte	pastry or pasta	*Véronique*	garnished with grapes
pâte brisée	shortcrust pastry		

Recipes